ACCESS 2000

ENI Publishing LTD

500 Chiswick High Road
London W4 5RG

Tel: 020 8956 2320
Fax: 020 8956 2321

e-mail: publishing@ediENI.com
http://www.eni-publishing.com

Collection directed by Corinne HERVO

MOUS
Access 2000

CREATING FORMS AND REPORTS

DESIGN VIEW

QUERIES

This book is the ideal tool for an effective preparation of the Access 2000 exam. The MOUS logo on the cover guarantees that this edition has been approved by Microsoft®. It contains the theoretical information corresponding to all the exams themes and you can test your knowledge by working through the practice exercises. If you succeed in completing these exercises without any difficulty, you are ready to take your exam. At the end of the book, you can see a list of the Access 2000 exam objectives, and the number of the lesson and exercise that refer to each of these objectives.

What is the Microsoft Office User Specialist certification?

The Microsoft Office User Specialist exam gives you the opportunity to obtain a meaningful certification, recognised by Microsoft®, for the Office applications: Word, Excel, Access, PowerPoint, and Outlook. This certification guarantees your level of skill in working with these applications. It can provide a boost to your career ambitions, as it proves that you can use effectively all the features of the Microsoft Office applications and thus offer a high productivity level to your employer. In addition, it would be a certain plus when job-seeking: more and more companies require employment candidates to be Microsoft Office User Specialist certificate holders.

What are the applications concerned?

You can gain Microsoft Office User Specialist certification in Office 97 applications (Word, Excel, PowerPoint and Access) and in Office 2000 applications (Word, Excel, PowerPoint, Access and Outlook). Microsoft Office User Specialist exams also exist for Word 7 and Excel 7. Two exam levels are offered for Word 97, Word 2000, Excel 97 and Excel 2000: a Core level (proficiency) and a second Expert level. For PowerPoint 97 and Access 97, only the Expert certification is available. For PowerPoint 2000, Access 2000 and Outlook 2000, only one level of certification is available.

If you obtain the Expert level for Word 97, Excel 97, PowerPoint 97 and Access 97, you are certified as a Master in Office 97. If you obtain the Expert level for Word 2000 and Excel 2000 as well as Microsoft Office User Specialist certification in PowerPoint 2000, Access 2000 and Outlook 2000, you are certified as a Master in Office 2000.

How do you apply to sit the exams?

To enrol for the exams, you should contact one of the Microsoft Authorized Testing Centers (or ATC). A list of these centres is available online at this address: http://www.mous.net. Make sure you know for which version of the Office application you wish to obtain the certificate (is it the 97 or 2000 version?).

There is an enrolment fee for each exam.

On the day of the exam, you should carry some form of identification and, if you have already sat a Microsoft Office User Specialist exam, your ID number.

What happens during the MOUS exam?

During the exam, you will have a computer that you must use to perform a certain number of tasks on the software in question. Each action you perform to carry out these tasks will be tested in order to make sure that you have done correctly what was asked of you. There are no multiple-choice questions and the exam is not a simulation; you work directly in the application (Word, Excel…).

You are allowed no notes, books, pencils or calculators during the exam. You can consult the application help, but you should be careful not to exceed the exam's time limit.

Each exam is timed; it lasts in general between 45 minutes and one hour.

How do you pass the exam?

You must carry out a certain percentage of the required tasks correctly, within the allocated time. This percentage varies depending on the exam.

You will be told your result as soon as you have finished your exam. These results are confidential (the data are coded) and are only made known to the candidate and to Microsoft.

What happens then?

You will receive a Microsoft-approved exam certificate, proving that you hold the specified Microsoft Office User Specialist level.

What happens if I fail?

You will be given the list of tasks that were not performed correctly, so you see where you went wrong. You can take the exam as many times as you like, but will have to pay the enrolment fee again each time you apply.

How this book works

This book is the ideal companion to an effective preparation of the **MOUS Access 2000** exam. It is divided into several sections, each containing one or more **chapters**. Each section deals with a specific topic: the Access working environment, managing databases and the objects they contain, working with tables and defining their relationships, working with records and the data stored in tables, creating forms and reports then managing their controls and sections and creating queries to select, delete and update information. Each chapter is independent from the others. You can work according to your needs: if you already know the techniques for working with records, for example, you can skip this lesson and go straight to the practice exercise for that chapter, then if you feel you need some extra theory, you can look back at the relevant points in the lesson. You can also study the lesson and/or work through the exercises in any order you wish.

At the end of the book, there is an **index** to help you find the explanations for any action, whenever you need them.

From theory...

Each chapter starts with a **lesson** on the theme in question and the lesson is made up of a variable amount of numbered topics. The lesson should supply you with all the theoretical information necessary to acquire that particular skill. Example screens to illustrate the point discussed enhance the lesson and you will also find tips, tricks and remarks to complement the explanations provided.

...To practice

Test your knowledge by working through the **practice exercise** at the end of each chapter: each numbered heading corresponds to an exercise question. A solution to the exercise follows. These exercises are done using the documents on the CD-ROM accompanying the book, that you install on your own computer (to see how, refer to the INSTALLING THE CD-ROM instructions). In addition to the chapter exercises, six **summary exercises** dealing with each of the section themes are included at the end of the book. The solutions to these exercises appear as documents on the CD-ROM.

All you need to succeed!

When you can complete all the practice exercises without any hesitation or problems, you are ready to sit the Microsoft Office User Specialist exam. In the table of contents for each chapter, the topics corresponding to a specific exam objective are marked with this symbol: ▦. At the back of the book, you can also see **the official list of the Access 2000 exam objectives** and for each of these objectives the corresponding lesson and exercise number.

The layout of this book

This book is laid out in a specific way with special typefaces and symbols so you can find all the information you need quickly and easily:

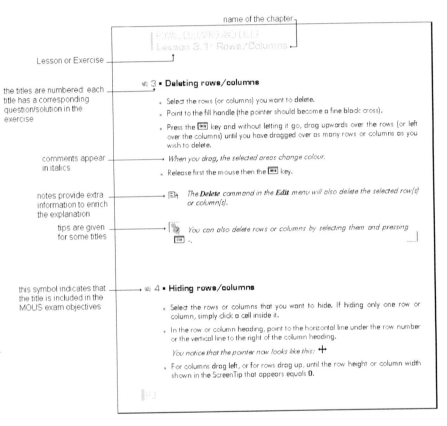

You can distinguish whether an action should be performed with the mouse, the keyboard or with the menu options by referring to the symbol that introduces each action: 🖰, ⬡ and 🗔.

Installing the CD-ROM

The CD-ROM provided contains the documents used to work through the practice exercises and the summary exercise solutions. When you follow the installation procedure set out below, a folder called MOUS Access 2000 is created on your hard disk and the CD-ROM documents are decompressed and copied into the created folder.

- Put the CD-ROM into the CD-ROM drive of your computer.
- Start the Windows Explorer: click the **Start** button, point to the **Programs** option then click **Windows Explorer**.
- In the left pane of the Explorer window, scroll through the list until the CD-ROM drive icon appears. Click this icon.

The contents of the CD-ROM appear in the right pane of the Explorer window. The documents you are going to be working on in the exercises appear in their compressed form MOUS Access 2000.exe, but you can also find them in the Summary and Practice Exercises folders.

- Double-click the icon of the **MOUS Access 2000** file in the right pane of the Explorer window.

*The **MOUS Access 2000** dialog box appears.*

- Click **Next**.

The installation application offers to create a folder called MOUS Access 2000.

- Modify the proposed folder name if you wish then click **Next**. If several people are going to be doing the practice exercises on the same computer, you should modify the folder name so each person is working on their own copy of the folder.

- Click **Yes** to confirm creating the **MOUS Access 2000** folder.

  The installation application decompresses the documents then copies them into the created folder.

- Click **Finish** when the copying process is finished.

- When the copy is finished, click the ⊠ button on the **Explorer** window to close it.

  You can now put away the CD-ROM and start working on your Microsoft Office User Specialist exam preparation.

MANAGING DATABASES
Lesson 1.1: Overview

1 ▪ Starting/leaving Microsoft Access 2000

Starting Access 2000

* Click the **Start** button on the taskbar.
* Drag up to the **Programs** option.
* Click the **Microsoft Access** option.

Access asks you if you want to create a new database or open an existing one.

* If you want to create a **Blank Access database**, activate the corresponding option. If you want the help of a wizard, activate the **Access database wizards, pages, and projects** option.

* If you wish to open an existing database, double-click the database name or click the **More Files** option if you need a database that does not appear in the list.

* If you want to start Access without either creating a new database or opening one, click the **Cancel** button.

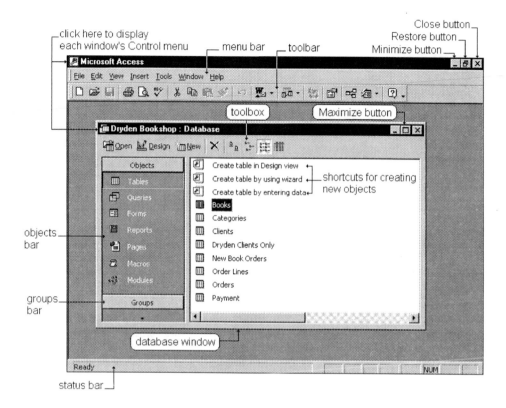

click here to display
each window's Control menu — menu bar — toolbar

Close button
Restore button
Minimize button

*A shortcut to the application, in the form of an icon, may be installed on your Windows Desktop. If this is the case, double-click the **Microsoft Access** icon to start the application.*

Leaving Access 2000

▪ **File - Exit** or click the ⊠ button on the application window or [Alt][F4]

▪ If you try to leave Access without saving any changes you have made to open objects, an error message appears. To save your changes and leave Access, click **Yes**, to leave Access without saving the changes, click **No** or to not save but keep Access open, click **Cancel**.

2 ▪ Using the Office Assistant

Asking the Office Assistant for help

- To display the Office Assistant, use the **Help - Show the Office Assistant** command.

- To ask the Assistant for help, click it.

- Click one of the help topics offered by the Assistant to see the corresponding help text or enter a search keyword in the text box and click the **Search** button.

  *A list of points relating to your search topic appears. The **See more** option shows another screen of topics, if one is available.*

- Click the required topic to see the help text.

- When you have finished consulting the help text, click the ☒ button to close the window.

- To hide the Office Assistant, use **Help - Hide the Office Assistant**. To display it again, click 🔲.

  When a light bulb appears next to the Office Assistant, Access has a useful tip to show you. Click the Assistant if you wish to see the tip.

Changing the look of the Office Assistant

- Click the 🔲 tool button or click the Assistant to show its search window then click the **Options** button.

- Click the **Gallery** tab and use the **Back** and/or **Next** buttons until you see the Assistant you require then click **OK**.

- If necessary, insert the Microsoft Office 2000 CD into the CD-ROM drive and click **OK** again to confirm changing the Assistant.

Below you can see **Practice Exercise** 1.1. This exercise is made up of 2 steps. If you do not know how to complete one of the steps, go back to the lesson to refer to the corresponding title. When you have finished, check your work by reading the **Solution** on the next page.

Steps that are likely to be tested in the exam are marked with a ▦ symbol. It is however recommended that you follow the whole exercise in order to gain a complete understanding of the lesson.

☞ **Practice Exercise 1.1**

1. Start the Microsoft Access 2000 application but do not create or open any databases.

▦ 2. Display the Office Assistant then show the help text that deals with creating forms. Close the help window then hide the Office Assistant.

If you want to put what you have learned into practice on a real document, you can work on summary exercise 1 for the MANAGING DATABASES section that can be found at the end of this book.

It is often possible to perform a task in several different ways, but here only the most efficient solution is presented. You can go back to the lesson if you wish to see the other techniques that can be used.

Solution to Exercise 1.1

1. To start the Microsoft Access 2000 application, click the **Start** button on the taskbar. Drag up to the **Programs** option and click the **Microsoft Access** option. Click the **Cancel** button to look at the workscreen without opening or creating any databases.

2. To display the Office Assistant, use the **Help - Show the Office Assistant** command.
   To see the help text that deals with creating a form, click the Assistant (if its search window is closed), enter the text **create a form** in the text box and click the **Search** button. Next, click the topic called **Create a form**. If necessary, click the ▢ button to maximize the **Microsoft Access Help** window and when you have read the help text, close the window by clicking the ✕ button.
   To hide the Assistant, right-click it and choose the **Hide** option.

MANAGING DATABASES
Lesson 1.2: Databases

1 ▪ Creating a database

Microsoft Access 2000 is a relational database management system that works in a Windows environment. Microsoft Access is used to manage data relating to a particular subject, such as stock control, personnel records etc while working within a single database file. In this file, related data are stored in tables and these tables are linked by a system of common fields. The links, or relationships between tables allow you to create objects (forms, queries, reports and so on) that can bring together information stored in several different tables.

What are the objectives of your database?

Before sitting down to start creating your database, you should first think carefully about why you are creating it and what the aim of your database is.

- What information will you be managing with the database and what should you place in each table? For example, one table may contain the list of product categories, with a description, an illustration and so on; another may contain all the articles. Linking these two tables by means of a category code would allow you to work simultaneously (in a report, for example) with the product information and the category information.

- Try to avoid repeating the same information from one table to another. For example, in a table listing each customer order made, it is not necessary to repeat the client information (name, address and so on), as you will have to fill in the same fields each time an order is placed. Entering this type of data several times wastes time and disk space and produces mistakes. It would make more sense to create a client code and to use that code to identify the orders: the orders and clients tables could then be linked so as to produce the client information only when needed, such as when order slips or invoices are printed. You can see why you should carefully plan which tables need to be linked and by which element.

- You should also note what documents you wish to produce from the information stored, such as printed lists (products, customers etc), statistics, charts, calculations and so on.

Database objects

Within the database file there is a group of objects, each contributing to how you manage the information in the database. Some objects are used to enter information in the database (tables, forms, data access pages) and others are used to retrieve or print the data entered (queries, reports).

Table Each table in a database contains data relating to a particular subject in the form of a datasheet.
For example, a Clients table may contain a company's customer list, a Products table would be a list of the articles distributed by the company, and so on. The table is the fundamental element of a database: every query, form or report has to be based on one or more tables.

Query Queries extract data from one or more tables and display their results in the form of a datasheet as a table does.
For example, a query can pick out rapidly from a Clients table the clients who live in a given town.

Form This object is used to enter and modify data in a table. In general a form shows one record at a time.
For example, a Clients form could be used to enter each client's address in a specially designed window.

Report A report is used to define the way in which data from a table are presented for printing including various calculations, if required.

Page Data access pages are Web pages used to add, modify or view data in a Microsoft Access database or a database in another application (such as Excel).

Macro This type of object is used to run a series of actions automatically, such as opening a form, displaying a toolbar etc.

Module Module objects contain procedures developed in the Visual Basic for Applications programming language, which can increase the amount of automated features and procedures within Access.

Creating a database without a wizard

* Activate the **Blank Access database** option in the dialog box that appears when you start Access or, if you are in the database window, use the **File - New** command or  or Ctrl **N**.

* Click the **General** tab then double-click the **Database** icon.

* Select the folder where you want to store the database then give the database a name in the **File name** text box

* Click the **Create** button.

A new database window appears on the screen:

* You can then create each object that will make up the database and define the relationships between the tables.

Creating a database with the Database Wizard

* Activate the **Access database wizards, pages, and projects** option in the dialog box that appears when you start Access and click **OK** or, if you are in the database window, use the **File - New** command or 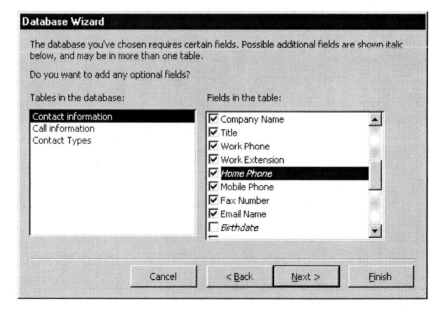 or ⌃Ctrl **N**.

* Click the **Databases** tab, if it is not active.

* Double-click the icon that corresponds to the type of database you wish to create, or select it and click **OK**.

* Select the folder where you want to store the database then give the database a name in the **File name** text box.

* Click the **Create** button.

  *The **Database Wizard** window opens and tells you what type of information can be stored in this database.*

* Click **Next** to go to the next step.

- In the **Tables in the database** list, click each table in succession and in the **Fields in the table** list, tick any extra fields (those in italics) you wish to add to the tables. Fields that are already ticked cannot be deselected as they are necessary for the construction of the chosen database.

- Click **Next** then choose a style for the presentation of the data entry windows (forms) in the database. If you click each option, a preview of the style's effects appears.

- Click **Next** then choose a style for the presentation of reports. If you click each option, a preview of the style's effects appears.

- Click **Next** then enter the title for the database in the corresponding text box. If you want a picture to appear on all the reports, tick the **Yes, I'd like to include a picture** option and click the **Picture** button to select one.

- Click **Next** then if you wish, leave the **Yes, start the database** option active. This ensures that once the database has been created, a **Main Switchboard** window appears on the screen. When this happens, the database window is minimized to an icon and you simply click one of the switchboard options to go to the corresponding action (adding or displaying records, viewing reports and so on). If you deactivate this option, the database window appears and you must work directly within it.

  *You can at any time display the **Main Switchboard** window again by clicking **Forms** in the objects bar on the database window then double-clicking the **Switchboard** form.*

- Click the **Finish** button.

  *The **Database Wizard** dialog box briefly appears on the screen to tell you how far it has progressed in creating the database and its objects.*

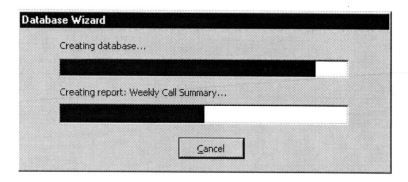

- If the **Yes, start the database** option is not active, Access tells you when it has finished creating the database. Click **OK** to view the database window. If the option was active, the **Main Switchboard** window appears directly on the screen.

2 ▪ Opening/closing a database

Opening a database

- Activate the **Open an existing file** option in the dialog box that appears when you start Access or, if you are in the database window, use the **File - Open** command or ⌷ or ⌷Ctrl⌷ **O**.

  By default Access assumes you want to open a database in the My Documents folder.

- To specify where the database you wish to open is located, click one of the shortcut buttons on the **Places Bar** on the left of the dialog box or open the **Look in** list.

- Go to the folder containing the database you want to open by double-clicking the folder icon.

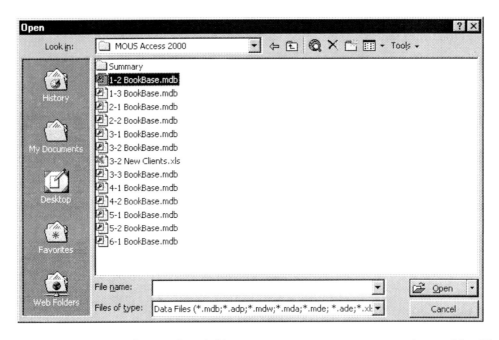

The **.mdb** (Microsoft DataBase) file extension may or may not be visible. The buttons seen are the same on the **Open** dialog box of every Microsoft Office 2000 application.

* To open a database, double-click its name or select it and click the **Open** button.

The database window appears inside the Microsoft Access 2000 application window.

A list of the last four databases used can be found at the base of the **File** menu.

Whatever the active window, you can go into the database window at any time by clicking the ⊞ tool button.

Closing a database

* **File - Close** or click the ☒ button on the database window.

🗐3 ▪ Backing up and restoring a database

* It is essential to make a backup copy of your database onto another storage medium (a floppy disk, tape or another workstation). You should update such backups regularly.
  To do this, you can use automatic backup to tape or another type of backup tool (such as MS Backup) or, failing that, copy the database file with the Windows Explorer.

* If your database is damaged or significant amounts of incorrect or unwanted data have been entered, you can replace it with the backup copy of the database using the corresponding backup tool or by recopying the backup database file with the Windows Explorer.

🗐4 ▪ Compacting and repairing a database

Database compaction and repair are combined into a single action. Compacting a database reduces the amount of space it takes up on the disk. When you delete data and/or objects in a database, it may become fragmented, which means it takes up more space than it should. Compacting will also repair a database if it is damaged.

* **Tools - Database Utilities**

* Click the **Compact and Repair Database** option.

  If a database is open, the compacting process begins immediately.

* If no database is open, select the database you wish to compact and click the **Compact** button.

- Give a name, a drive and a folder for the compacted version of the database and click the **Save** button.

If you specify the same name, drive and folder, the compacted database will replace the original one.

 You can interrupt the compacting process by pressing Ctrl Break *or* Esc.

*If you want a database to be compacted and repaired automatically when it is closed, activate the **Compact on Close** option in the **Options** dialog box (**Tools - Options - General** tab).*

Below you can see **Practice Exercise** 1.2. This exercise is made up of 4 steps. If you do not know how to complete one of the steps, go back to the lesson to refer to the corresponding title. When you have finished, check your work by reading the **Solution** on the next page.

Steps that are likely to be tested in the exam are marked with a ⊞ symbol. It is however recommended that you follow the whole exercise in order to gain a complete understanding of the lesson.

☞ Practice Exercise 1.2

⊞ 1. Using the Database Wizard, create a new database called **1-2 Suppliers.mdb**. Choose the wizard called **Contact Management** and save the database in the **MOUS Access 2000** folder.
The **Home Phone** field should be added to the **Contact information** table, the style used for the database windows should be **Stone** and the style used for the reports should be **Corporate**.
Give **Supplier Names** as the title of your database and finish by opening the database.

2. Open the **1-2 BookBase.mdb** database, which is in the **MOUS Access 2000** folder.
Close this database again.

⊞ 3. Make a backup copy of the **1-2 BookBase.mdb** database, which is in the **MOUS Access 2000** folder into the folder called **Summary** that is also in the **MOUS Access 2000** folder.

4. Without opening it, compact the **1-2 BookBase.mdb** database (in the **MOUS Access 2000** folder). Name the compacted version of the database **1-2 BookBaseComp.mdb** and save it in the **MOUS Access 2000** folder.

If you want to put what you have learned into practice on a real document, you can work on summary exercise 1 for the MANAGING DATABASES section that can be found at the end of this book.

It is often possible to perform a task in several different ways, but here only the most efficient solution is presented. You can go back to the lesson if you wish to see the other techniques that can be used.

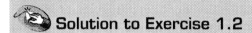

Solution to Exercise 1.2

1. To create a new database called 1-2 Suppliers in the MOUS Access 2000 folder, with the help of the Database Wizard, click the ⬜ button, then the **Databases** tab then double-click the **Contact Management** icon. Enter **1-2 Suppliers** in the **File name** text box. If necessary, open the **Save in** list and select the drive containing the MOUS Access 2000 folder then double-click the **MOUS Access 2000** folder to open it. Click the **Create** button. Click the **Next** button. Select the **Contact information** table in the **Tables in the database** list, then in the **Fields in the table** list, activate the field called **Home Phone**.
Click **Next**. Select **Stone** in the list of display styles and click **Next** again. Select **Corporate** from the printing styles shown then click **Next** again.

   In the **What would you like the title of the database to be?** text box, enter **Supplier Names** then click the **Next** button. Make sure the **Yes, start the database** option is active then click the **Finish** button.

2. To open the 1-2 BookBase.mdb database in the **MOUS Access 2000** folder, use the **File - Open** command. Open the **Look in** drop-down list and find the drive in which you copied the items from the CD-ROM accompanying this book. Double-click the **MOUS Access 2000** folder then the **1-2 BookBase.mdb** file.
To close this database, click the ⊠ button on the database window.

3. To make a backup copy of the 1-2 BookBase.mdb database into the Summary folder (which is inside the MOUS Access 2000 folder), start by clicking the **Start** button on the Windows taskbar. Drag up to the **Programs** option and choose the **Windows Explorer** option.
Click the **MOUS Access 2000** folder then the **1-2 BookBase.mdb** file. Click the Copy tool button, choose the folder called **Summary** then click the Paste tool button.

4. To compact the 1-2 BookBase.mdb database (in the MOUS Access 2000 folder) without opening it, use the **Tools - Database Utilities** command and choose the **Compact and Repair Database** option. If necessary, open the **Look in** list and select the drive containing the **MOUS Access 2000** folder then double-click that folder to open it. Select the **1-2 Book-Base.mdb** database and click the **Compact** button. Enter **1-2 BookBase-Comp.mdb** in the **File name** text box then click the **Save** button.

MANAGING DATABASES
Lesson 1.3: Database objects

1 ▪ Modifying the display of objects in the database window

⁜ You can modify the way the objects are displayed in the database window. To do this, click one of the following tools:

shows the objects as large icons.

shows the objects as small icons.

shows a list of the object names.

shows a detailed list.

The chosen type of display is applied to all the database objects (tables, queries etc).

*The same options appear in the **View** menu, as well as the **Arrange Icons** option, which sorts the list of objects according to various criteria (by type, by date and so on).*

2 ▪ Managing objects

⁜ To select an object, click the type of object that interests you in the objects bar. The corresponding list of objects appears in the database window. Click the name of the object you want to select. Another way to select the object is to type its name.

⁜ To save the structure, or design, once you have modified it in Design view, use **File - Save** or 🖫 or ⌃ **S**. If necessary, give the object a name then click **OK**.

*You can also save your changes when you close an object's window. The **File - Save As** command is used to save the object under a different name.*

⁜ To delete a database object, select it in the database window and press the Del key. If necessary, click the **Yes** button to confirm deleting the object.

*If you prefer not having to confirm the deletion of database objects, deactivate the **Document deletions** option in the **Options** dialog box (**Tools - Options - Edit/Find** tab).*

■ To hide an object (so its name no longer appears in the database window), select it then use **View - Properties** or [icon]. Activate the **Hidden** option then click **OK**.

The hidden object is no longer visible in the list of objects.

■ To make a hidden object reappear, show all the hidden objects by activating the **Hidden objects** option in the **Options** dialog box (**Tools - Options - View** tab) then modify the object's properties to deactivate the **Hidden** property.

■ To rename an object, select it in the database window, click the object name again then type in the new name and press the [↵] key. You can also change an object's name by right-clicking the object and choosing the **Rename** option or using the **Edit - Rename** command or [F2].

The list is sorted again automatically into alphabetical order.

■ To copy an object, select it and use the **Edit - Copy** command or [icon] or [Ctrl] **C**. This copies the selected object into a part of the Windows memory called the clipboard.

You can then paste the contents of the clipboard using the **Edit - Paste** command or [icon] or [Ctrl] **V**.

If you try to copy an object that has the same name as another object in the same place, Access will ask you to rename the copy. In this case, give the new name and click **OK**.

3 ▪ Saving an object as a Web page

You would save an object as a Web page if you wanted to publish on the Internet and/or an intranet. This type of page can only be viewed by the network user.

▪ In the database window, click the name of the object you wish to export.

▪ **File - Export**

▪ Open the **Save as type** list and select the **HTML Documents (*.html;*.htm)** option.

▪ If required, modify the **File name** in the corresponding text box.

▪ Select the drive then the folder in which you wish to save the document.

▪ Click the **Save** button.

4 ▪ Going into an object's design (Design view)

You can modify an object's design, or structure, while it is in Design view.

▪ If you are in the database window, select the object and click the button.

If you are in Form or Datasheet view, click the ⬚▾ tool button.

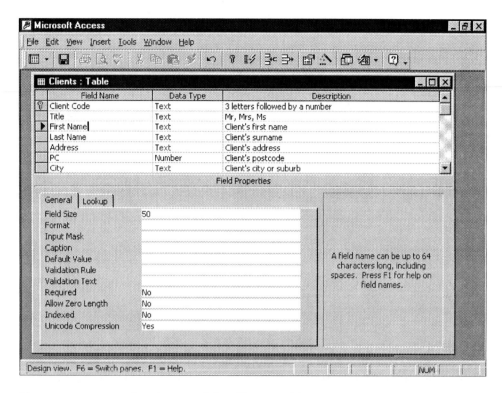

Here you can see the design of the Clients table.

※ To return to Datasheet view, click the [image] tool button. To return to Form view, click the [image] tool button.

Below you can see **Practice Exercise** 1.3. This exercise is made up of 4 steps. If you do not know how to complete one of the steps, go back to the lesson to refer to the corresponding title. When you have finished, check your work by reading the **Solution** on the next page.

Steps that are likely to be tested in the exam are marked with a ▦ symbol. It is however recommended that you follow the whole exercise in order to gain a complete understanding of the lesson.

☞ Practice Exercise 1.3

To work through exercise 1.3, open the ***1-3 BookBase.mdb*** database located in the ***MOUS Access 2000*** folder.

1. Show the database objects in the form of a detailed list then show the names as a simple list again.

▦ 2. Delete the query called **List of clients** and rename the **Enter Books** form as **Enter Book Details**.

▦ 3. Save the **Books** table as a Web page. This Web page should be stored in the **MOUS Access 2000** folder under the name of **Book List**.

▦ 4. Go into the design of the **Enter Book Details** form then display it in Form view.

If you want to put what you have learned into practice in a real document you can work on summary exercise 1 for the MANAGING DATABASES section that can be found at the end of this book.

It is often possible to perform a task in several different ways, but here only the most efficient solution is presented. You can go back to the lesson if you wish to see the other techniques that can be used.

Solution to Exercise 1.3

1. To show the database objects in the form of a detailed list, click the 🔲 tool button. Then, click the 🔲 tool button to show the names as a simple list again.

2. To delete the query called List of clients, click **Queries** in the objects bar then select the **List of clients** query. Press the Del key then if necessary, click the **Yes** button to confirm the deletion.
   To rename the Enter Books form, click **Forms** in the objects bar then select the **Enter Books** form. Click the name of the **Enter Books** form again; type **Enter Book Details** then press ↵.

3. To save the Books table as a Web page, click **Tables** in the objects bar, select the **Books** table then use the **File - Export** command. Open the **Save as type** list and choose the **HTML Documents (*.html;*.htm)** option. Next, enter **Book List** in the **File name** text box. If necessary, open the **Save in** list and select the drive containing the **MOUS Access 2000** folder and double-click this folder to open it. Finish by clicking the **Save** button.

4. To go into the design of the Enter Book Details form, click **Forms** in the objects bar, select the **Enter Book Details** form and click the 🔲 Design button.
   To show this form in Form view, click the 🔲 tool button.

MANAGING DATABASES
Exercise 1.3: Database objects

TABLES
Lesson 2.1: Table design

1 ▪ Creating a table in a database

Preparing to create a table

▪ A table is a set of data organised with a particular structure, or **design**.
This design is based on one fundamental element: the **field**.
Each field in the table represents a particular category of information (a Surname field contains a list of names, a Postcode field contains postal or zip codes and so on).

Each set of fields (along with the data they contain) makes up a **record** (in a Clients table, for example, each record is the set of information referring to a single customer). Each record in the table is designed to contain the same pieces of information, even though some records may have fields that are not filled in.

This set of data is brought together in a table, consisting of columns (the fields) and rows (the records).

Clients : Table						
Client code	**Title**	**First Name**	**Last Name**	**Address**	**PC**	**City**
ALD01	Mr	Richard	Alderson	56 Harvey Rd	8520	Tewesbury
AND01	Ms	Suzanne	Anderley	67 Milton Road	8630	Abbeyville
AND02	Ms	Berenice	Andrews	27 Ridley St	5250	St Lucia
BAR01	Mrs	Linda	Barnett	38 Harrison Cres	7520	Moreton
BLA01	Mr	Curtis	Blake	35 Nichol St	9520	Killybill
BUR01	Mr	James	Burton	37 Chambers St	4100	Eastport
CHA01	Ms	Wendy	Chang	C/ Dunes Hotel, 9 Espl	8580	Keaton Hill
CHA02	Mrs	Mavis	Charles	29 Bartlett Cres	6530	Lorton
CLI01	Mrs	Margaret	Cliff	29 William St	8615	Rafter
CRA01	Ms	Tina	Crayton	77 Kennedy Drive	8615	Rafter
DEL01	Ms	Gillian	Deller	13 Read Road	8580	Keaton Hill
DOR01	Mrs	Michelle	Dorcas	10 Kings Ct	4150	Beecham
DRE01	Ms	Joanne	Drew	78 Abbey Road	8630	Abbeyville
EGA01	Mr	Patrick	Egan	35 Prior St	6510	Stoughton
FED01	Ms	Lisa	Federicks	159 George St	4120	Oak Grove

Record: ◄◄ ◄ 1 ► ►► ►* of 52

※ While in a table's design, you can name the fields on which it is based and determine the properties of those fields, such as the type of data they should contain (text, numbers, dates?) and the maximum number of characters that can be entered (the field length).

One of the fields in the table should give each record a unique identity. This is the **primary key** (if you do not define one, Access can do so and manage the data it contains automatically).

Creating a table with a wizard

※ Click **Tables** in the objects bar then double-click the **Create table by using wizard** shortcut that appears in the list of tables.

You can also click the [New] *button, select the* **Table Wizard** *option and click* **OK**.

※ Select the type of table you wish to create: **Business** or **Personal**.

※ Select one of the **Sample Tables** that is closest to the table you had in mind.

※ Indicate which fields you wish to include in the table:

- for each field you are inserting, select it in the **Sample Fields** list and click the [>] button.

- to insert all the fields in the list, click [>>].

- to remove a field from the list, select it in the **Fields in my new table** list and click the [<] button.

- to remove all the fields from this list, click [<<].

The selected fields now appear in the **Fields in my new table** *list.*

※ If you are not happy with the names of some of the fields, you can rename them: click the name concerned in the **Fields in my new table** list then click the **Rename Field** button. Type the new name into the text box and click **OK**.

You can always subsequently modify the field names if those suggested by Access are unsuitable or add other fields to the table, if you wish.

※ Click the **Next** button to go to the next step in the wizard.

※ Give the table a name and indicate how the primary key is to be defined:

- if you want Access to create an AutoNumber type field (whose value will be incremented automatically), activate the first option,

- activate the second option if you want to define the primary key yourself.

※ Click **Next**.

※ If you are defining the primary key yourself, specify which field to use and the type of data it will contain then click the **Next** button.

※ Click the **Relationships** button if you want to define the relationship that exists between the table you are creating and one or more existing tables. Click **Next**.

※ Specify what you want to do next with the new table then click the **Finish** button.

Creating a table without using a wizard

※ Click **Tables** in the objects bar then double-click the **Create table in Design view** shortcut that appears in the list of objects.

You can also click the ⊞ New button, select the **Design View** option then click **OK**.

※ For each field you want to insert in the table:

- click in the first empty cell in the **Field Name** column and enter the name of the field. You can use between 1 and 64 characters, except for full stops (.), exclamation marks (!), an accent grave (`) and square brackets ([]).

- select the **Data Type** that you wish the field to accept. To choose a type, click the corresponding cell in the **Data Type** column, open the drop-down list then click the required type:

Text	alphanumerical characters (letters and/or numbers); the length of a text field is limited to 255 characters.
Memo	alphanumerical characters; the length of a Memo field is limited to 65535 characters.

Number	any numbers, with or without decimal points.
Date/Time	dates or times (Access controls the validity of the dates and times you enter).
Currency	the values are presented in a currency format, in accordance with your regional settings (e.g. £1,050.00 or $1,050.00).
AutoNumber	a numerical value, incremented automatically when a new record is entered.
Yes/No	only two items are allowed in this sort of field: Yes or No. For example, a field called Paid would only show whether a bill has been paid (Yes) or not (No).
OLE Object	this type of field is used to insert into the table various objects made in other Windows applications.
Hyperlink	this type of field contains text used to make a hyperlink.
Lookup Wizard	starts a wizard that creates a field in which the field value is selected ("looked up") in a field in another table or in a list of values which you define.

- If necessary, enter the **Description** of the field contents in the corresponding column. This text appears on the status bar when you add or modify data in that field.

Field Name	Data Type	Description
Book Number	AutoNumber	Catalogue number
Title	Text	Book title
Author	Text	Author's name
Category Code	Text	Three-letter code
Retail Price	Number	Price including tax
▶ Description	Memo	Brief description of the book's theme

Field Properties

General | Lookup

Format	
Caption	
Default Value	
Validation Rule	
Validation Text	
Required	No
Allow Zero Length	No
Unicode Compression	Yes

A field name can be up to 64 characters long, including spaces. Press F1 for help on field names.

* To define the properties of each field, click the row of that field then fill in the lower part of the window.

  How to modify field properties is described later in this chapter.

* If necessary, specify which field is to be the primary key: click the corresponding row then click the [🔑] tool button.

* Save the table's design with the **File - Save** command or [💾] or [Ctrl] **S**.

* If required, close the table using **File - Close**.

📄 *The name of a table can contain up to 64 characters.*

44

2 ▪ Modifying a table's design

* Click **Tables** in the objects bar, select the table whose structure you wish to modify and click the ![Design] button.

* To insert a field, select the row below where you wish to insert it, press [Insert] or click the ![tool button] tool button then give the characteristics of the field.

* To delete a field, select the corresponding row then press [Del] or click the ![tool button]. tool button. Click **Yes** to confirm the deletion.

  All the data within the field will be lost.

* To rename a field, select the name in the **Field Name** column, press the [Del] key then enter the new name.

* To move a field, click the corresponding field selector then drag the field row into its new position.

* To modify the **Data Type** allowed, select the new type in the drop-down list.

  The data must be convertible from one type to another; the most common types of conversion are:

  - from a Number, Currency or Date/Time type to Text (and inversely providing the textual data has been entered in a format compatible with the Number, Currency or Date/Time types),

  - from a Number to a Currency type (and vice versa),

  - from a Text to a Memo type; Memo to Text is possible but if the values in the Memo field are longer than 255 characters, they will be cut off.

  - You cannot convert an AutoNumber type field.

  If you modify a field used to establish a relationship between two tables, the relationship will be deleted automatically.

» Click the 🖫 tool button to save the changes made to the table's design.

» Close the table with the **File - Close** command.

> *If a form is associated with the table, remember to carry over the changes into the form. Any new forms or reports created from the table will take into account the modified structure of the table.*
>
> *You can also modify the structure of a table in Datasheet view. In this view you can delete or move columns (fields), insert new ones or rename the existing columns (by double-clicking the column header).*

▣3 ▪ Modifying field properties

Each field has property values, which are the various characteristics that define the field. The available properties differ depending on the data type of the selected field (Text, Number, AutoNumber, Date/Time etc).

» Click **Tables** in the objects bar and select the table containing the field whose properties you wish to modify. Click the 🖳 Design button.

» Click the field whose properties you want to change.

*The properties of the selected field appear in the lower part of the window. In the example below, you can see the properties of a field with **Text** type data.*

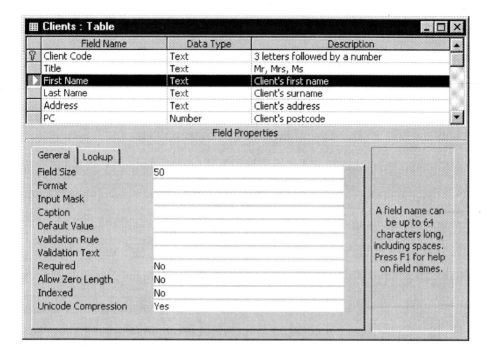

- Click the text box of the property in question and make your changes:

Field Size For a Text type field; specify the number of characters that can be entered (up to 255).

For a Number type field; open the drop-down list then select the required size for the field.

Format For Number, Currency, Date/Time or Yes/No type fields; open the drop-down list and select one of the preset formats or enter a custom format if none of the preset formats are suitable.

For Text or Memo type fields; create a custom format using special characters (for example, the ">" symbol places all the characters entered in upper case letters and the "<" symbol puts them all in lower case letters).

Decimal Places For Number or Currency type fields; open the drop-down list then select the required number of decimal places for the selected field.

Input Mask	For Text, Number, Currency and Date/Time type fields; this property uses special characters to control how data can be entered in the field. You can define an input mask yourself or by using a wizard (to do this, click ▨), but an input mask created with a wizard can only be used for Text or Date fields. For example, you can create an input mask for a client code that would oblige you to enter three letters followed by three numbers (the mask would be **LLL000**: **L** means you must enter a letter and **0** means you must enter a number). You can see the list of characters that you can use to make an input mask by clicking the **Input Mask** property then pressing F1. When **Input Mask** and **Format** properties have been defined on the same field, the **Format** property has prevalence and the input mask is ignored.
Caption	For all field types; you can enter a text that will replace the name of the field when it is displayed in a datasheet, a form or a report.
Default Value	For all field types (except OLE Object and AutoNumber); you can specify the value that will appear automatically in the field when you enter a new record ; the user can accept this value or enter another one.
New Values	For AutoNumber type fields; open the drop-down list then select one of the two options proposed. These determine how the field value is incremented when a new record is added to the table.
Validation Rule	For all field types except OLE Object and AutoNumber; you can enter an expression that limits the values that can be entered in the field. For example you could create an expression for a Title field that would force you to enter either Mr, Mrs or Miss: in the **Validation Rule** property this expression would be **Mr or Mrs or Miss**.

Validation Text	For all field types except OLE Object and AutoNumber; enter a text that would appear in an error message if the data entered in the field did not correspond to the **Validation Rule** property. If you define the **Validation Rule** property without defining a **Validation Text**, Microsoft Access displays a standard error message when the field data does not meet the validation rule.
Required	For all field types except AutoNumber; if you want to make it compulsory to enter a value in this field when a new record is created, open the drop-down list and choose **Yes**. **No** is the default for this property.
Allow Zero Length	For Text, Memo or Hyperlink type fields; open the drop-down list and choose **Yes** if you wish to allow zero-length strings in the field (this is symbolised by " " : a zero-length string means there is deliberately no value entered in that field). The **No** option is selected by default.
Indexed	For all field types except Memo, Hyperlink and OLE Object; you can index a field by choosing **Yes (Duplicates OK)** or **Yes (No Duplicates)** in the drop-down list. Access will find records more quickly during a search, or when running a query or a sorting operation. When you index a table by a field, Microsoft Access stores the values from that field "to one side", establishing a link with the records in the table. When you make a search in that field, Microsoft Access does not look in the table (which contains all the values in all the fields) but only in the list of indexed values, producing a faster result. Because the index and the table are still linked, the record corresponding to the indexed value is found rapidly. Access automatically indexes a table's primary key (no duplicates allowed).

Unicode Compression	For Text, Memo or Hyperlink type fields; if you select **Yes**, any character whose first byte equals 0 could be compressed during storage and decompressed during retrieval. This applies to all characters in Western European languages such as English, French or Spanish. Microsoft Access 2000 uses the Unicode character coding system; in this system, each character is represented by 2 bytes (instead of one as in previous versions of Access). This means that Text, Memo or Hyperlink fields require more storage space than previously. Unicode compression can reduce the amount of space needed.

※ Click the ▣ tool button to save the changes made to the properties.

※ If necessary, close the table with the **File - Close** command.

To read the help text concerning a particular property, click the property and press F1 *.*

▤4 ▪ Creating a lookup column

In a lookup column you can select the values you need instead of typing them in. The values used for this type of field can either be defined when you create the field or can be looked up in another table or query (hence the name of this type of field!).

Using a list of fixed values

You need to state what values will be available in the list.

※ Click **Tables** in the objects bar, select the table concerned then click the ▥ Design button.

※ Enter the **Field Name** in the corresponding column or click its row if it already exists.

※ Click the field's **Data Type** column, open the drop-down list then select the **Lookup Wizard** option.

*The **Lookup Wizard** window appears on the screen.*

※ Activate the **I will type in the values that I want** option then click the **Next** button to go to the next step.

※ Give the **Number of columns** required for the list in the corresponding text box then click the first empty cell in the **Col1** column

※ Enter the values for the list as in a datasheet: the 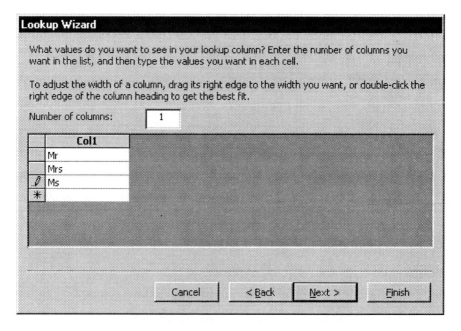 key takes you to the next cell.

Lookup Wizard

What values do you want to see in your lookup column? Enter the number of columns you want in the list, and then type the values you want in each cell.

To adjust the width of a column, drag its right edge to the width you want, or double-click the right edge of the column heading to get the best fit.

Number of columns: 1

	Col1
	Mr
	Mrs
🖉	Ms
✳	

| Cancel | < Back | Next > | Finish |

※ Click the **Next** button to go to the next step.

※ Enter the text for the field label in the text box and click the **Finish** button.

* To view the lookup column's properties, click the **Lookup** tab in the lower part of the window. The **Row Source Type** is a **Value List** and the values in the list appear in the **Row Source** property, separated by semi-colons. The number of columns can be seen in the **Column Count** property.

* Click the tool button to save the changes made to the table.

* If necessary, close the table with the **File - Close** command.

Using a list of data from another table

The lookup column will contain values from a field in an existing table or query.

* Click **Tables** in the objects bar, select the table concerned then click the button.

* Enter the **Field Name** in the corresponding column or click its row if it already exists.

* Click the field's **Data Type** column, open the drop-down list then select the **Lookup Wizard** option.

  *The **Lookup Wizard** window appears on the screen.*

* Activate the first option so the values can be looked up in another table or query then click the **Next** button.

* In the **View** frame, activate the option that corresponds to the type of object you wish to choose.

* In the list, select the table or query that contains the values you wish to insert then click the **Next** button.

* Select the field(s) whose values should appear in the lookup column then click the **Next** button.

* Deactivate the **Hide key column (recommended)** option if you want to see the column containing the primary key values.

* If necessary, modify the width of the list's columns then click the **Next** button.

* If necessary, select the field in which you wish to store the value then click **Next**.

- Enter the text for the lookup column's label then click the **Finish** button.

- To view the lookup column's properties, click the **Lookup** tab in the lower part of the window. The **Row Source Type** is listed as **Table/Query**. The **Row Source** property contains an SQL statement that selects the fields inserted in the list. The number of columns can be seen in the **Column Count** property.

- Click the [💾] tool button to save the changes made to the table.

- If necessary, close the table using the **File - Close** command.

⊞5 ▪ Using the Input Mask Wizard

An input mask provides a preset format to make data entry easier.

- Click **Tables** in the objects bar, select the table concerned then click the [Design] button.

- Select the field for which you want to define an input mask, click the **Input Mask** property then the [...] button.

   This wizard will offer you a certain number of preset input masks.

- Choose the required mask in the **Input Mask** column.

- To test the mask, click the **Try It** text box and enter some data.

- Click the **Next** button.

- If required, modify the contents of the input mask box if you want to customise the mask. You can use certain symbols to represent required or optional letters and digits.

- Next, if you wish, modify the character in the **Placeholder character** list box. This character will appear in the text box when you start entering data and will be replaced by your values when you type them in.

- If necessary, click the **Try It** text box then enter some data to test the changes made to the input mask.

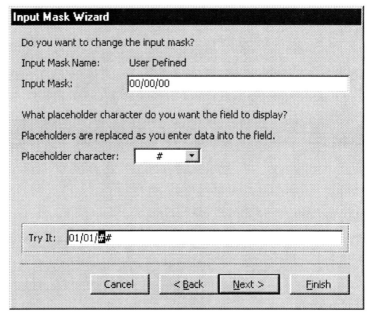

» Click **Next** then the **Finish** button.

» Click the 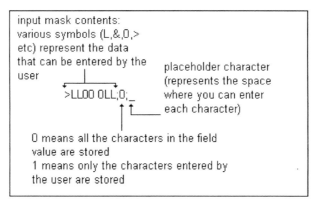 tool button to save the changes made to the table.

» If necessary, close the table using the **File - Close** command.

In the property sheet, the input mask can be made up of three parts, each separated by a semi-colon:

input mask contents:
various symbols (L,&,0,>
etc) represent the data
that can be entered by the
user

placeholder character
(represents the space
where you can enter
each character)

>LL00 0LL;0;_

0 means all the characters in the field
value are stored
1 means only the characters entered by
the user are stored

6 ▪ Defining one or more primary keys

*Each table in a database should include a field or set of fields that gives each record a unique identity: this is called the **primary key**.*

▪ Click **Tables** in the objects bar, select the table for which you wish to define a primary key then click the 📐 Design button.

The primary key can only be defined while you are in the structure of the table (Design view).

▪ If the primary key is to use a single field, select the corresponding row. If the primary key uses several fields, select the rows that correspond to the various fields (use the Ctrl key if the rows are not adjacent).

A primary key can be made up of more than one field when you cannot ensure that the values in a single field will all be different.

▪ Click the 🔑 tool button.

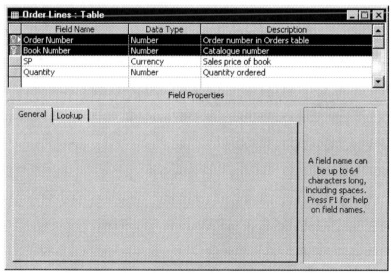

A key symbol appears on each selected row.

- Click the tool button to save the changes made to the table.

- If necessary, close the table using the **File - Close** command.

Below you can see **Practice Exercise** 2.1. This exercise is made up of 6 steps. If you do not know how to complete one of the steps, go back to the lesson to refer to the corresponding title. When you have finished, check your work by reading the **Solution** on the next page.

All the steps in this exercise are likely to be tested during the exam.

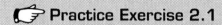

Practice Exercise 2.1

*To work through exercise 2.1, open the **2-1 BookBase.mdb** database located in the **MOUS Access 2000** folder.*

1. Create the **Books** table, without the help of a wizard, using the table below to guide you:

Field Name	Data Type	Description
Book Number	AutoNumber	Catalogue number
Title	Text	Book title
Author	Text	Author's name
Category Code	Text	Three-letter code
Retail Price	Number	Price including tax
Description	Memo	Brief description of the book's theme

The **Book Number** field is to be the primary key.

2. Modify the design of the **Books** table in the following ways:

- insert the **Number of Pages** field, with a **Number** data type, underneath the **Retail Price** field.
- move the **Description** field underneath the **Category Code** and **Retail Price** fields.
- choose a **Currency** data type for the **Retail Price** field.

Save the changes made to the design of the **Books** table when you have finished.

▦ 3. Modify the properties of certain fields in the **Books** table as described below:

- make it compulsory to enter data in the **Title**, **Category Code** and **Retail Price** fields.
- the size of the **Category Code** field should be set to **3** characters
- only values higher than zero should be allowed in the Retail Price field. If an invalid value is entered, the error message **Please enter a value greater than 0!** should appear.
- create a custom format for the **Author** field so the text appears in capital letters.

Save the changes made to the **Books** table and close it.

▦ 4. Create a lookup column containing the values **Mr**, **Mrs** and **Ms** for the **Title** field in the **Clients** table. Use the word **Title** as the label for this lookup column.
Finish by saving the changes made to the **Clients** table.

▦ 5. Using the wizard, create an input mask for the **Contact Date** field in the **Clients** table. Choose a **Short Date** type of input mask and make the # symbol the placeholder character which will be seen in the text box when you start entering data.
Save the changes made to the **Clients** table then close it.

▦ 6. In the **Order Lines** table, define a primary key, made up of the fields **Order Number** and **Book Number**.
Save the changes made to the **Order Lines** table and close it.

If you want to put what you have learned into practice in a real document you can work on summary exercise 2 for the TABLES section that can be found at the end of this book.

It is often possible to perform a task in several different ways, but here only the most efficient solution is presented. You can go back to the lesson if you wish to see the other techniques that can be used.

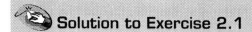 **Solution to Exercise 2.1**

1. To create the Books table as described in the exercise, click **Tables** in the objects bar then double-click the **Create table in Design view** shortcut that appears in the list of tables.

   In the first cell of the first row, enter **Book Number** as the field name then open the **Data Type** drop-down list and select the **AutoNumber** option. In the **Description** column, enter the text **Catalogue number**.

   In the first cell of the second row, enter **Title** as the field name. Next, open the **Data Type** drop-down list and select the **Text** option. In the **Description** column, enter the text **Book title**.

   In the first cell of the third row, enter **Author** as the field name then open the **Data Type** drop-down list and select the **Text** option. In the **Description** column, enter the text **Author's name**.

   In the first cell of the fourth row, enter **Category Code** as the field name. Open the **Data Type** drop-down list and select the **Text** option. In the **Description** column, enter the text **Three-letter code**.

   In the first cell of the fifth row, enter **Retail Price** as the field name then open the **Data Type** drop-down list and select the **Number** option. In the **Description** column, enter the text **Price including tax**.

   In the first cell of the sixth row, enter **Description** as the field name. Next, open the **Data Type** drop-down list and select the **Memo** option. In the **Description** column, enter the text **Brief description of the book's theme**.

   To set the Book Number field as the primary key, click the row of the **Book Number** field then click the [key] tool button.

Click the ▣ tool button, enter **Books** in the text box then click **OK**.

2. To insert a Number of Pages field underneath the Retail Price field, select the **Description** field row and press the Insert key. Enter **Number of Pages** in the first cell of the new row then open the **Data Type** drop-down list and select the **Number** option.

To move the Description field between the Category Code and Retail Price fields, start by clicking the row selector at the **Description** field. Next, drag this field until the black horizontal line that appears is positioned underneath the **Category Code** field.

To choose a Currency data type for the Retail Price field, open the **Data Type** drop-down list for the **Retail Price** field and choose the **Currency** option.

To save the changes made to the design of the **Books** table, click the tool button.

3. To transform the Title, Category Code and Retail Price fields into required fields (i.e you must enter a value in them), click the **Required** property for each of these fields and choose the **Yes** option.

To modify the size of the Category Code field to 3 characters, click the row for the **Category Code** field then enter **3** in the **Field Size** property.

To ensure that only values higher than zero are entered in the Retail Price field, select the field then click the **Validation Rule** property and enter **>0**. The message "Please enter a value greater than 0!" must appear if the value entered in the Retail Price field is not higher than zero: to ensure this, click the **Validation Text** property and type the text **Please enter a value greater than 0!**.

To make the text in the Author field appear in capital letters, select the **Author** field then click in the **Format** property and type the **>** symbol.

To save and close the **Books** table, click the [🖫] tool button then use the **File - Close** command.

4. To create a lookup column containing the values Mr, Mrs and Ms for the Title field in the Clients table, start by clicking **Tables** in the objects bar.

Select the **Clients** table and click the [Design] button. Click the **Data Type** column for the **Title** field, open the drop-down list and choose the **Lookup Wizard** option.

Activate the **I will type in the values that I want** option then click the **Next** button to go to the next step. Click the first empty cell in the **Col1** column and type **Mr**. Press the [⇥] key and type **Mrs** then press [⇥] again and type **Ms** and click **Next**.

Check that **Title** appears as the label for this list then click the **Finish** button.

To save the changes made to the **Clients** table, click [🖫].

5. To create an input mask with the wizard, for the Contact Date field in the Clients table, click the **Contact Date** field row. Click the **Input Mask** property and click the [⋯] button

Choose **Short Date** in the **Input Mask** list then click **Next**. Next, select the # character in the **Placeholder character** list box and click **Next** then the **Finish** button.

To save and close the Clients table, click the [🖫] tool button then use the **File - Close** command.

6. To define the primary key in the Order Lines table, first click **Tables** in the objects bar. Select the **Order Lines** table and click the [Design] button. Select the rows corresponding to the **Order Number** and **Book Number** fields and click the tool button.

To save and close the Order Lines table, click the tool button then use the **File - Close** command.

TABLES
Lesson 2.2: Relationships between tables

TABLES
Lesson 2.2: Relationships between tables

1 ▪Establishing a relationship between two tables

Different types of relationships between tables

Creating a relationship between tables in your database allows you to analyse, at one glance, data stored in different places, and to use that data more efficiently. For example, you want to produce a report containing the name of each item you produce, and also the category it belongs to: your report would be based on a query which joins the two tables. The tables are joined by the primary key of one of them. Between two tables, three types of relationship are possible, which are created and managed differently:

- the "**one-to-many**" relationship: a record in the primary table can have several matching records in the related table (the primary table contains the primary key by which the tables are joined).
  For example: one category has several corresponding items:

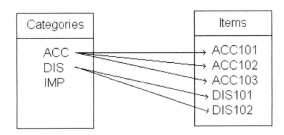

Each Category code is matched with many Item codes (many arrows "leave from" a single Category code), but each Item code is matched with just one Category code.

- the "**many-to-one**" relationship is the same sort of relationship but in reverse. For example: several orders may be placed by the same client:

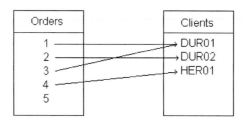

An order number can only match one client, but the same client code appears in several orders. Although these two relationships seem to be the same, they cannot be managed in the same way. The direction of the relationship depends on which table is the primary table.

- In a "**many-to-many**" relationship, a record in the primary table can match many records in the related table, and a record in the related table can correspond to many records in the primary table.
  For example: one order contains many different items, and one item can figure in many different orders. The many-to-many relationship can be represented by this type of schema:

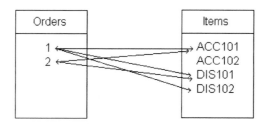

One order number matches several item codes, and one item code has several corresponding order numbers.
To manage this type of relationship correctly, you should split it into a "one-to-many" relationship, and a "many-to-one" relationship.

- The "**one-to-one**" relationship: one record in the primary table matches a single record in the related table, and vice-versa. This type of relationship is rare as the two tables would ordinarily be combined into a single table. The only sort of circumstance where you might meet this type of relationship is when the related table contains temporary data to be deleted later (it is easier to delete a superfluous table than to delete a few fields from an all-inclusive table).

Establishing a relationship between two tables

You must relate the tables by the primary key field of the primary table, and the corresponding field in the related table. Tables can be related providing they have a field in common (even if its name is not the same in the two tables) and that these fields contain the same type of data.

※ If you are in the database window, activate the **Tools - Relationships** command or click the ⬚ tool button.

*When you go into the **Relationships** window for the first time in the active database, the window is empty and Access prompts you to add tables to it.*

※ Select the tables between which you wish to create relationships. Use the ⌈Shift⌋ key to select adjacent tables or the ⌈Ctrl⌋ key if they are not adjacent.

※ Click the **Add** button.

※ When all the necessary tables have been added, click the **Close** button.

*The tables appear in the window but as yet no relationships have been established. The **Relationships** window is used to display and define all the existing relationships between tables and queries in the active database.*

※ To establish a relationship between the tables, drag the field which is common to both from the primary table towards the related table.

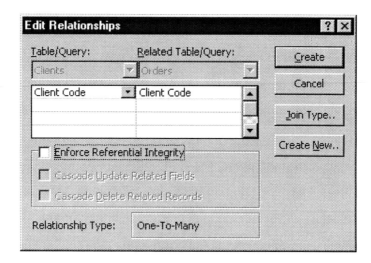

You define the relationship's attributes in the dialog box illustrated above.

▪ Activate the **Enforce Referential Integrity** option if you want Access to ensure the compatibility of the data in the two tables. It does this by checking that corresponding data exists in the primary table every time you add a record to the related table, and by refusing to delete a record from the primary table if it has one or more matched records in the related table.

▪ Even if you have activated the referential integrity option, you can still modify the primary key, or delete records from the primary table, provided you activate the **Cascade Update Related Fields** and/or **Cascade Delete Related Records** option(s). In the first case, Access will update all the related records so that they take account of the changes in the primary key; in the second, Access deletes any record related to the one you deleted.

▪ Click the **Create** button.

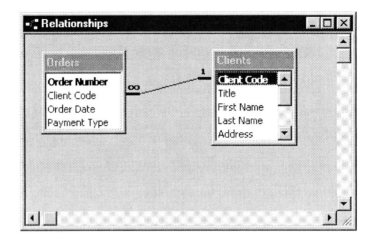

You can see the join line linking the two tables: The **1** and **∞** symbols show what type of relationship has been established, and the thick lines indicate referential integrity.

* Click the tool button to save the relationship you have defined.

* Click the ☒ button on the **Relationships** window to close it.

To see the contents of the **Relationships** window again, click .

It is not possible to delete a primary table, nor to change the data type of a field used in a join, nor to delete such a field.

You can only establish one relationship between the same two tables.

2 ▪ Managing relationships in a database

* If you are in the database window, click the tool button to open the **Relationships** window.

If the **Relationships** window is empty, Access prompts you to add tables or queries.

* To add one or more tables to the **Relationships** window, use the 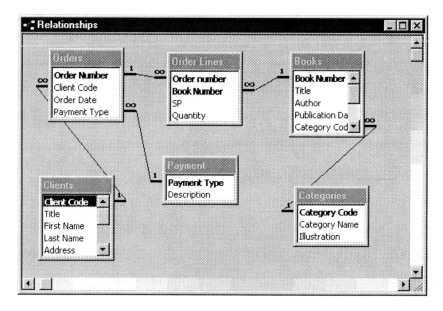 tool button. Select the tables, click the **Add** button then click **Close**.

* To remove one of the tables from the window, click its title bar then use the **Relationships - Hide Table** command (or click the table and press `Del`. To clear the entire contents of the window, use the **Edit - Clear Layout** command.

  Be careful. Simply removing a table from the relationships window does not delete its relationships with other tables.

* To move a table, drag the title bar of the table in question to its new position. Release the mouse when you are happy with its new position.

* To go into the design of a table, right-click the table concerned and choose the **Table Design** option.

* If you wish to edit the relationship characteristics, double-click the join line then make the required changes and click **OK**.

  To delete a relationship, click the join line once then press the `Del` key.

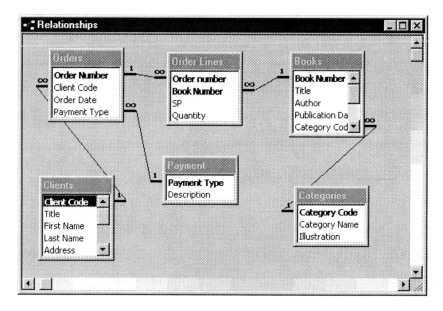

TABLES

Lesson 2.2: Relationships between tables

- After you have modified the contents of the **Relationships** window, click the tool button to save them then click the ⊠ button on the window to close it.

3 ▪ Showing/modifying linked data in a subdatasheet

*When two tables are linked by a **one-to-many** relationship, the rows from the table on the "many" side can be seen in a subdatasheet for each corresponding row in the table on the "one" side.*

- Click **Tables** in the objects bar then double-click the name of the table in which you wish to display or modify the linked data.

The table is opened in Datasheet view and in the column to the left of each row a + sign appears.

- To show (and if you wish modify) the linked data for one or more rows (records), click the + sign for the row(s) concerned.

*On the example below, you can see the lines from the **Orders** table that relate to the Client Code **EGA01**. When the subdatasheet is open, the + sign becomes a - sign.*

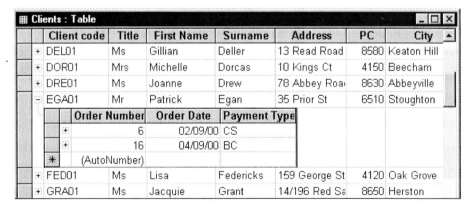

- To hide the data linked to a row, click the - sign next to that row.

- Close the datasheet by clicking the ⊠ button in the top right corner of it.

⊞4 ▪ Printing database relationships

▪ If you are in the database window, click the ⊞ tool button to open the **Relationships** window.

▪ **File - Print Relationships**

The database relationships appear in a report, with the same layout as seen in the relationships window.

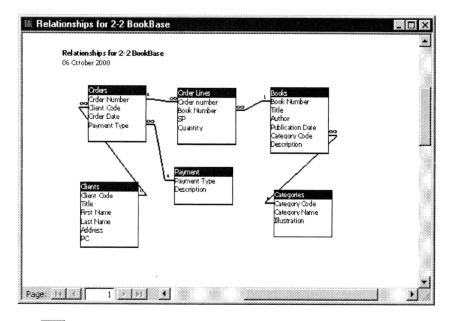

▪ Click the 🖨 tool button to print the relationships.

▪ Click the ⊠ button to close the report window. You can choose to save the report by clicking the **Yes** button or click **No** if you wish to close it without saving.

▪ Close the relationships window by clicking the ⊠ button, in the top right corner of the window.

TABLES
Exercise 2.2: Relationships between tables

Below you can see **Practice Exercise** 2.2. This exercise is made up of 4 steps. If you do not know how to complete one of the steps, go back to the lesson to refer to the corresponding title. When you have finished, check your work by reading the **Solution** on the next page.

Steps that are likely to be tested in the exam are marked with a ▦ symbol. It is however recommended that you follow the whole exercise in order to gain a complete understanding of the lesson.

👉 **Practice Exercise 2.2**

*To work through exercise 2.2, open the **2-2 BookBase.mdb** database located in the **MOUS Access 2000** folder.*

▦ 1. Establish relationships between the **Clients** and **Orders** tables and also between the **Books** and **Order Lines** tables. For each relationship, you should enforce referential integrity and allow fields to be updated.

2. Insert the **Categories** table into the relationship window and establish a relationship between the **Categories** and **Books** tables, applying referential integrity and allowing for field updates.
Move the **Categories** table underneath the **Books** table.
Modify the relationship between the **Payment** and **Orders** tables so as to allow field updates. To finish, save and close the relationship window.

▦ 3. In the **Clients** table, show the linked data for the client named **Patrick Egan** as a subdatasheet. Read the data shown in the subdatasheet then close the Clients table.

▦ 4. Print the database relationships then close the report window without saving it. Finish by closing the relationship window.

If you want to put what you have learned into practice in a real document you can work on summary exercise 2 for the TABLES section that can be found at the end of this book.

It is often possible to perform a task in several different ways, but here only the most efficient solution is presented. You can go back to the lesson if you wish to see the other techniques that can be used.

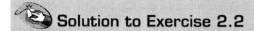

Solution to Exercise 2.2

1. To establish the relationships described in step 1 of the exercise, start by clicking the ⬚ tool button.

   To establish a relationship between the Clients and Orders tables, drag the **Client Code** field from the **Clients** table onto the **Client Code** field in the **Orders** table. Activate the **Enforce Referential Integrity** and **Cascade Update Related Fields** options then click the **Create** button.

   To establish a relationship between the Books and Order Lines tables, drag the **Book Number** field from the **Books** table onto the **Book Number** field in the **Order Lines** table. Activate the **Enforce Referential Integrity** and **Cascade Update Related Fields** options then click the **Create** button.

2. To insert the Categories table into the relationship window, click the ⬚ tool button. Select the **Categories** table, click the **Add** button then click **Close**.

   To establish a relationship between the Categories and Books tables, drag the **Category Code** field from the **Categories** table onto the **Category Code** field in the **Books** table. Activate the **Enforce Referential Integrity** and **Cascade Update Related Fields** options then click the **Create** button.

   To move the Categories table under the Books table, drag the title bar of the **Categories** table until the table is underneath the **Books** table.

   To modify the relationship between the Payment and Orders tables so that fields can be updated, double-click the join line between the **Payment** and **Orders** tables. Activate the **Cascade Update Related Fields** option and click **OK**.

To save and close the relationship window, click the [■] tool button then click the [✕] button in the top right corner of the relationship window.

▦ 3 To show the linked data for Patrick Egan in the form of a subdatasheet, start by selecting **Tables** in the objects bar and double-click the **Clients** table. Click the + sign that appears on the row corresponding to the client **Patrick Egan** (client **EGA01**). Once you have read the linked data, choose the **File - Close** command.

▦ 4. To print the database relationships, click the [▣] tool button to open the relationship window then choose the **File - Print Relationships** command and click the [🖶] tool button.

To close the report window without saving it, click the [✕] button in the top right corner of the window then click the **No** button.

To close the relationship window, click the [✕] button in the top right corner of the window.

MANAGING DATA
Lesson 3.1: Records

MANAGING DATA
Lesson 3.1: Records

📖 1 ▪ **Entering records in a datasheet**

- To enter records in a table's datasheet, click **Tables** in the objects bar then double-click the name of the table to which you wish to add new records.
  To enter records in a form's datasheet, click **Forms** in the objects bar then double-click the name of the form you wish to use to add new records. Next open the drop-down list on the [🖉 ▾] tool button and choose **Datasheet View**.

- Click the [▸∗] button in the bottom left of the screen to create a new record.

  You can also click the [▸∗] tool button on the toolbar.

- Fill in the first field in the record and confirm with [↵] or press [⇥] to go to the next field or the next record.

  In a datasheet, the symbols you see to the left of the first column are called **record selectors**: *the pencil symbol indicates that the record is being modified and that the changes made have not yet been saved, and the star represents a new record.*

- Each field in the record is entered in the same way. If you press [Esc] you delete the contents of the last field entered in the current record. If you press [Esc] a second time, you delete the contents of all the fields in the current record.

- Use the following shortcuts to insert certain field values:

[Ctrl] ;	to insert the current date.
[Ctrl] :	to insert the current time.
[Alt] [Ctrl] [Space]	to insert that field's default value.
[Ctrl] '	to insert the value from the same field in the previous record.
[Ctrl] [↵]	to make a line break in the cell.

  When the pencil disappears from the record selector column, the data has been saved on the disk. This is automatic and you do not need to do anything to save your data.

* Close the datasheet by clicking the button on the datasheet window or with the **File - Close** command.

2 ▪ Managing the datasheet

Selecting rows or columns in a datasheet

* Show the table in Datasheet view.

* To select a row or column, click the row selector or the field selector (the column header).

* To select a group of rows or columns, select the first row or column and drag over the others to spread out the selection.

* To select all the rows or all the columns, click the square in the top left corner of the datasheet (where the rows and columns meet).

The selected rows and columns appear in a different colour.

📄 *To cancel the selection, click elsewhere in the datasheet.*

Modifying the column width/row height

* Display the table in Datasheet view.

* Select the columns or rows concerned, if you want to modify several at once.

* Point to the vertical line to the right of the field selector or the horizontal line beneath the row selector for the column or row you wish to modify.

The pointer appears as a double-headed arrow.

* Drag with the mouse to move the line and when it is in the desired position, release the mouse button.

You cannot have varying row heights in the one datasheet. As soon as you modify the height of one row (or a selection of rows), the heights of all the rows in the datasheet are adjusted automatically.

*You can also modify the row height/column width by using the **Row Height** and **Column Width** command in the **Format** menu.*

If you wish to fit the width of a column to its widest visible entry, double-click the vertical line to the left of the column.

Freezing columns

Frozen columns remain on the screen while you scroll through other columns further away.

* Display the table in Datasheet view.
* Select the columns you wish to freeze.
* **Format - Freeze Columns**
* You can cancel this layout with the **Format - Unfreeze All Columns** command.

Frozen columns will also appear on every printed page if the width of the printout is larger than the physical width of the paper.

Hiding/showing certain columns

* Display the table in Datasheet view.
* **Format - Unhide Columns**

The names of the columns that are visible in the datasheet have their check boxes ticked.

* Deactivate or activate the check box for any column you wish to hide or show.

» When you have finished, click the **Close** button.

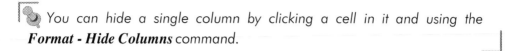 *You can hide a single column by clicking a cell in it and using the* ***Format - Hide Columns*** *command.*

Moving a column

» Display the table in Datasheet view.

» Select the column concerned.

» Click the field selector of the selected column and drag the column until the thick vertical line that appears is in the correct position.

» When you are happy with the column position, release the mouse button.

Saving a table's presentation

» Display the table in Datasheet view.

» Make your required changes to the presentation of the table.

» **File - Save** or 🖫 or ⌂Ctrl **S**.

This command saves certain presentation options such as the position of columns, the row height and the column width.

🗎 *The* ***Format - Font*** *command can be used to change the character font visible in the datasheet.*

▣3 ▪ Entering records with a form

※ Click **Forms** in the objects bar, select the name of the form in which you wish to enter the records and click the ▭ Open button. You can also open a form by double-clicking its icon.

The form opens and in it you can see one record. The active display is **Form View** *and it is in this view that you will enter the new records.*

※ Click the ▶* button in the bottom left corner of the form window or on the toolbar.

A blank form appears on the screen.

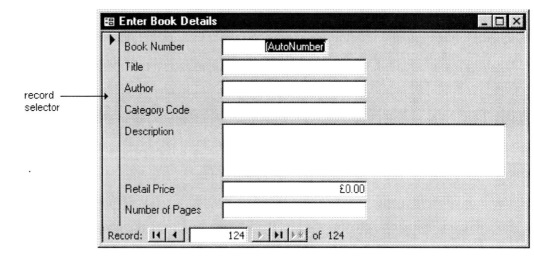

record selector

※ For each field in the record enter the required data then press the ↵ or ⇥ key to go to the next field or to the next record. You must respect the allowed data type for the field, as well as the field length.

In a form, the pencil symbol seen in the **record selector** *indicates that the record is being modified and that the modifications have not yet been saved on the disk.*

▪ Each field in the record is entered in the same way. If you press `Esc` you delete the contents of the last field entered in the current record. If you press `Esc` a second time, you delete the contents of all the fields in the current record.

▪ As when entering records in a datasheet, you can use shortcut keys to insert certain field values (cf. Entering records in a datasheet).

When the pencil disappears from the record selector column, the data has been saved on the disk. This is automatic and you do not need to do anything to save your data.

▪ Close the datasheet by clicking the ☒ button on the datasheet window or with the **File - Close** command.

4 ▪ Entering different types of data

▪ When entering data, use only the type of data allowed for that field and respect the field length as well as the following rules:

- when entering a number with decimal points, use the decimal point defined in the Windows **Control Panel** (usually a dot),

- when you fill in a Currency field, type in the field value without any formatting (do not enter a thousands separator or any currency symbol),

- when entering a date or time, use the format defined in the **Control Panel**,

- when filling in a Memo field, you can use `Shift` `F2` to show the **Zoom** window and view the entire text entered, no matter how small the text box is,

- you cannot fill in an AutoNumber type field as the corresponding number is automatically increased by Access,

- when filling in a Yes/No field, click the check box for **yes** or remove the tick for **no** (you can also do this by pressing the `Space` key),

- the contents of an OLE Object field cannot be entered on the keyboard as this field contains only objects inserted into the database,

- a hyperlink address can be made up of 4 parts, separated by a hash symbol: displaytext#address#subaddress#screentip. The first item is optional and corresponds to the text shown in a field or control. The second item corresponds to a full URL address or a UNC path to a document. The subaddress item refers to a location in the page or the file (such as a bookmark in a Word document or a slide number in a PowerPoint presentation). The screentip is the text that you see when you point to the hyperlink. You can also enter this type of field using **Insert - Hyperlink** or or Ctrl **K**.

5 ▪ Hiding existing records to enter new ones

▪ If you wish to add records directly into a table, open the table in Datasheet view. If you wish to add records by means of a form, open the form in Form view.

▪ **Records - Data Entry**

A blank form (or row in the datasheet) appears. You can see that this record is numbered 1: only the records you are going to enter are currently available.

▪ Enter the new records.

▪ To show all the records again, use the **Records - Remove Filter/Sort** command.

6 ▪ Moving within the records

Going to records/fields/data in Datasheet view

▪ Open the table, query or form concerned in Datasheet view ( ).

* Move around using the following buttons that are in the bottom left corner of the window:

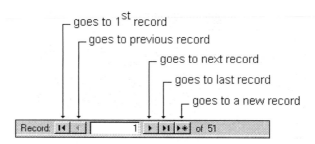

goes to 1st record
goes to previous record
goes to next record
goes to last record
goes to a new record

You can also slide the cursor on the vertical scroll bar until the number of the record required can be seen.

* To go to a visible record, click the corresponding row (use the scroll arrows to make it visible).

* To go to a specific record, double-click the record number seen in the bottom left corner of the window, enter the required number and confirm with ⏎.

* To select a piece of visible data (a word, a string of characters etc) within a field, use the usual Windows selection techniques: double-click a word to select it, drag to select several words or characters and so on.

* To select a whole field value, point to the vertical line to the left of the value and when the pointer takes the form of a thick white cross, click. Drag the cross over several cells to select several values.

* Use the following keys:

↓/↑	to go to the next/previous record.
Ctrl End / Ctrl Home	to go to the last field in the last record/the first field in the first record.
→/← or ⇥/Shift ⇥	to go to the next/previous field.
End / Home	to go to the last/first field of the current record.
PgDn / PgUp	to show the next screen down/last screen up.

`Ctrl` `PgDn`/`Ctrl` `PgUp`	to show the next screen to the right/to the left.
`Ctrl` `↓`/`Ctrl` `↑`	to go to the same field in the last/first record.
`F5`	to give the number of the record to which you want to go.

* Use the following techniques to select the field values or records:

`F2`	to select or deselect the current field (the one containing the insertion point).
`Ctrl` `Space`	to select an entire column when one of its values is selected.
`Shift` `Space`	to select a whole record when one of its fields is selected (`Shift` `↓` or `Shift` `↑` can then spread the selection to the adjacent records).

📄 *The **Edit - Go To** command options can also be used to go to certain records.*

Going to records/fields/data in Form view

* Open the form concerned in Form view (🔲▾).

* Use the `PgUp` and `PgDn` keys (or `Ctrl` `PgUp` and `Ctrl` `PgDn`) to scroll through the records.

* Use the `Ctrl` `End` or `Ctrl` `Home` keys to go to the last record or the first record.

* Use the `↑` or `↓` (or `⇥` and `Shift` `⇤`) keys to go from field to field or click a field label to select that field's value.

* Use the `F2` key to select or deselect the current field (the one where the insertion point is).

* Click the record selector to select the current record.

* To go to a specific record, press `F5`, enter the number and confirm with ↵.

* Press `Ctrl` **A** to select all the records.

*The corresponding options can be found in the **Edit** menu.*

■ To select visible data (words, characters etc) in a field, use the usual Windows selection techniques: double-click a word to select it, drag to select several words or characters and so on.

■ Click elsewhere in the form to cancel a selection.

7 ▪ Deleting records

Deleting one or more records in Datasheet view

■ Open the table or form concerned in Datasheet view ( ).

■ Select the rows of the records you wish to delete. If you only want to delete one record, click it.

■ **Edit - Delete Record** or or [Ctrl] -

■ Click the **Yes** button to confirm deleting the record(s).

■ If necessary, close the table or form by activating **File - Close**.

📄 *This action cannot be undone.*

If you select the whole row of a record, you can use the [Del] key to delete it.

🔍 *You can also use a **query** to delete in a single action all the records that meet a certain set of criteria.*

Deleting a record in Form view

▪ Open the form concerned in Form view (⊞ ▾).

▪ Display the record you wish to delete.

▪ **Edit - Delete Record** or ▶✕

▪ Click **Yes** to confirm the deletion.

▪ If necessary, close the form with the **File - Close** command.

> *You can also select the record by clicking the record selector (the vertical bar on the left of the form) and pressing the* Del *key.*

8 ▪ Sorting records rapidly

▪ Display in Datasheet view (⊞ ▾), the table, form or query containing the records you wish to sort.

▪ Click the field by which you wish to sort.

▪ Use these tool buttons:

A↓Z   to sort in ascending order.

Z↓A   to sort in descending order.

▪ To keep the active sort order, save the table by clicking the 💾 tool button.

▪ To return to the sort order defined by the primary key, use the **Records - Remove Filter/Sort** command.

89 ▪ **Filtering records**

Filters *temporarily limit which records are displayed in a datasheet or form.*

Filtering by a single criteria

▪ Open the form in Form view (⊞▾) or the table or query in Datasheet view (▦▾).

▪ Click the field value by which you want to filter the records: if only part of the field value is involved, select the corresponding characters.

▪ **Records - Filter - Filter By Selection** or ▼

▦ Clients : Table							_□✕
	Client code	**Title**	**First Name**	**Surname**	**Address**	**PC**	**City**
▶ +	BAR01	Mrs	Linda	Barnett	38 Harrison Cr	7520	Moreton
+	MAR02	Ms	Ruth	Martin	9/27 Thurston	7520	Moreton
+	SMI01	Mr	John	Smithers	15 Tall Tree Rc	7520	Moreton
+	STO01	Mrs	Lynn	Stoke	34 Barns Drive	7520	Moreton
*						0	

Record: ◄◄ ◄ 1 ► ►I ►✳ of 4 (Filtered)

Only the records that meet the selected criteria appear in the datasheet or form. The number of records filtered appears on the status bar.

▪ To keep the filter, save the object by clicking the 🖫 tool button: the next time you open the table, simply click the ▼ tool button to apply the filter.

▪ To show all the records again, remove the filter by using **Records - Remove Filter/Sort** or by clicking the ▼ tool button.

▸ To apply the last filter created, click the 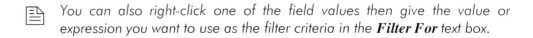 tool button again.

📄 *You can also right-click one of the field values then give the value or expression you want to use as the filter criteria in the **Filter For** text box.*

🖱 To show all the records except those that correspond to the active value, use the **Records - Filter - Filter Excluding Selection** command.

Filtering records by several criteria

▸ Open the form in Form view ( ) or the table or query in Datasheet view ( ).

▸ **Records - Filter - Filter By Form** or

The blank form on your screen is called the filter design grid. The criteria for the last filter you defined appear automatically.

▸ For each field concerned, give the filter criterion, either by typing in the data or by clicking in the field to open the list of values associated with it and selecting one.

Sort criteria can also contain comparison operators such as >, <, >=, <=, <> (unlike).

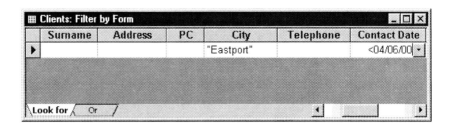

Any criteria relating to a Text type field are automatically placed in quotation marks.

When several criteria are given in the same filter design grid, Access filters the records that meet all the filter criteria simultaneously.

▪ To filter records meeting one of several sets of criteria, define the first set then click the **Or** tab at the bottom of the window.

A new blank form appears. The previously set criteria can be seen by clicking the **Look for** *tab.*

▪ Enter a second criteria set.

Access filters records that meet either the first or second set of criteria.

▪ When all the criteria have been set, click the ▽ tool button.

▪ To save the filter, save the current object by clicking the 🖫 tool button. The next time you open the table, query or form, you can reapply the filter automatically by clicking the ▽ tool button.

▪ To view all the records again, remove the filter with the **Records - Remove Filter/Sort** command or by clicking the ▽ tool button.

▪ To reapply the last filter created, click the ▽ tool button.

▪ To create another filter or modify the active filter, click the ▦ tool button then modify or delete the active criteria. To delete a set of criteria, click the corresponding tab then use the **Edit - Delete Tab** command. To delete all the sets of criteria, use the **Edit - Clear Grid** or click the ☒ tool button.

▪ To leave the filter design grid without keeping any changes made, click the ☒ button.

A filter (as with any sort order) is associated with a database object. You can save one filter with a form and a second one with the table's datasheet. However only one filter at a time can be associated with a particular object.

If you create a report or form based on a table or query which has an associated filter, the new report or form will also have the filter.

*The **Records - Filter - Advanced Filter/Sort** command can be used to create more complex filters or sort orders, as you would in a query design grid. If you choose this command, a design grid appears (much like the one used to create queries), which will contain the criteria corresponding to the active filter.*

Below you can see **Practice Exercise** 3.1. This exercise is made up of 9 steps. If you do not know how to complete one of the steps, go back to the lesson to refer to the corresponding title. When you have finished, check your work by reading the **Solution** on the next page.

Steps that are likely to be tested in the exam are marked with a ▦ symbol. It is however recommended that you follow the whole exercise in order to gain a complete understanding of the lesson.

☞ Practice Exercise 3.1

To work through exercise 3.1, open the ***3-1 BookBase.mdb*** database located in the ***MOUS Access 2000*** folder.

▦ 1. Enter the following records into the **Clients** table:

Client Code	Title	Surname	First Name	Address	Post-code	City	Telephone	Contact Date	Has Acct
LUC01	Mr	Lucian	Paul	14 Thorn St	4100	Eastport	555 7570	05/06/00	No
MAL01	Ms	Mallet	Karen	2 King Square	8615	Rafter	555 1498	07/07/00	Yes

2. Go to the datasheet for the **Clients** table and make the following changes:
   - increase the width of the **Address** column.
   - move the **First Name** column before the **Surname** column.
   - freeze the **Client Code** column.
   - save this layout and close the **Clients** table.

▦ 3. Using the **Enter Client Details** form, enter these two records then close the form:

Client Code	Title	First Name	Surname	Address	Post-code	City	Telephone	Contact Date	Has Acct
FUR01	Mrs	Esther	Furley	9 Clark St	4120	Oak Grove	551 0025	05/04/00	No
SAL02	Mr	Rhett	Salmon	10 Oak Lane	7520	Moreton	558 9154	04/07/00	No

4. Enter the data for the following two records, using the **Enter Book Details** form then close the form:

Book Number	Title	Author	Publication Date	Category Code	Description	Retail Price	Number of Pages	In Stock
(Auto Number)	Dead of Night	Reeves, Lynn	01/08/00	CRI	A serial killer stalks campus students	5.00	390	Yes
(Auto Number)	Call Me	Hunt, Kelly	02/08/00	FIC	Romance starts on a switchboard	6.00	385	No

5. Hide the existing records, add the following records to the **Payments** table, then display all the records before closing the table:

Payment Type	Description
AC	Account
BT	Book token

6. Open the **Clients** table in Datasheet view, carry out the actions described below then close the table:

- go to record **45** then go to the last field in this record,

- go to the same field (Has Account) in the last record.

- using the keyboard, select the record containing the active field then spread the selection to include the previous 3 fields.

7. Delete record number **110** from the **Enter Book Details** form then close the form.

8. Sort the records in the **Books** table by the **Title**, in ascending order, save the sort order and close the table.

9. Filter the records in the **Clients** table to find all the clients living in either **Eastport** or **Keaton Hill** whose contact date comes before **04/06/00** then close the Clients table, saving the filter.

If you want to put what you have learned into practice in a real document you can work on the summary exercise 3 for the MANAGING DATA section that can be found at the end of this book.

It is often possible to perform a task in several different ways, but here only the most efficient solution is presented. You can go back to the lesson if you wish to see the other techniques that can be used.

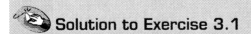
Solution to Exercise 3.1

1. To enter the records described in step 1 of the exercise, click **Tables** in the objects bar then double-click the icon of the **Clients** table.

   Click the ▶∗ button visible at the bottom of the window and type the data shown (press the ⇆ key after entering each piece of information).

2. To go to the datasheet of the Clients table, click **Tables** in the objects bar then double-click the **Clients** table icon.

   To widen the Address column, point to the vertical line on the right of the field selector for the **Address** column and drag this line to the right.

   To move the First Name column in front of the Surname column, select the **Surname** column by clicking its field selector. Next, drag the column header, until the thick vertical line that appears is positioned to the right of the **First Name** column.

   To freeze the Client Code column, select the **Client Code** column by clicking its field selector then use the **Format - Freeze Columns** command.

   To save the layout of the Clients table, click the 🖫 tool button. To close the table, use the **File - Close** command.

3. To enter the records described in step 3 of the exercise, using the Enter Client Details form, click **Forms** in the objects bar and double-click the **Enter Client Details** icon. Click the ▶* button that appears at the bottom of the window and type the data shown.

   To close the Enter Client Details form, use the **File - Close** command.

4. To enter the data described in step 4, using the Enter Book Details form, click **Forms** in the objects bar and double-click the **Enter Book Details** icon. Click the ▶* button at the bottom of the window and type the data shown.

   To close the Enter Book Details form, use the **File - Close** command.

5. To add the records described in step 5 to the Payments table, click **Tables** in the objects bar then double-click the **Payment** table icon. Next, use the **Records - Data Entry** command and type:

   AC, ⇆ **, Account,** ⇆ **, BT,** ⇆ **, Book token** and ⇆ .

   To display all the records again and close the payments table, use the **Records - Remove Filter/Sort** command followed by **File - Close**.

6. To open the Clients table in Datasheet view, click **Tables** in the objects bar then double-click the **Clients** table icon.

   To go to record 45, double-click the record number in the bottom left corner of the window and type **45** then press ↵ . Next, press the End key to go to the last field in that record.

   To go to the same field (Has Account) in the last record, press Ctrl ↓ .

   To select the record containing the active field, using the keyboard, press the Shift Space keys. Next, hold down the Shift key and press the ↑ key three times to include the 3 previous records in the selection.

   To close the Clients table, use the **File - Close** command.

7. To delete the record 110 from the Enter Book Details form, click **Forms** in the objects bar then double-click the icon of the **Enter Book Details** form.

Select the record number that appears in the bottom left corner of the form window then type **110** followed by ⏎. Next, click the record selector (the vertical bar on the left of the form), press the Del key then click **Yes** to confirm the deletion.

To close the Enter Book Details form, use the **File - Close** command.

8. To sort the records in the Books table in ascending order by Title, click **Tables** in the objects bar then double-click the **Books** table icon. Next, click the **Title** column and then the tool button.

To save the sort order and close the **Books** table, click the tool button then activate the **File - Close** command.

9. To filter the records in the Clients table in order to find all the clients living in either Eastport or Keaton Hill whose contact date comes before 04/06/00, click **Tables** in the objects bar and double-click the **Clients** table icon. Next, click the tool button. Open the drop-down list attached to the **City** field and select the **Eastport** value. Press the ⇆ key twice to access the **Contact Date** field and enter the expression **<04/06/2000**. To give a second set of criteria, click the **Or** tab. Open the drop-down list attached to the **City** field and select the **Keaton Hill** value. Press the ⇆ key twice to access the **Contact Date** field and enter the expression **<04/06/2000**. To finish, apply the filter by clicking the tool button.

To close the Clients table, keeping the filter, use the **File - Close** command and click the **Yes** button.

MANAGING DATA
Lesson 3.2: Data

▣1 ▪ Copying/moving data with the Office Clipboard

*You can use the **Office Clipboard** to copy and paste multiple items, unlike the **Windows Clipboard** which can only hold one item at a time.*

▪ Open the object containing the data you wish to copy or move.

▪ Show the **Clipboard** toolbar with the **View - Toolbars - Clipboard** command or right-click one of the visible toolbars and choose the **Clipboard** option.

*The **Clipboard** toolbar is unavailable in views where the **Copy**, **Cut** and **Paste** commands are not available.*

This toolbar may appear automatically once two consecutive copies are made.

▪ For each item you wish to copy or move:

- select the item; if it is in another application other than Microsoft Access 2000, go into that application.

- to move the item, use the **Edit - Cut** command or [✂] or [Ctrl] **X**; to make a copy, use the **Edit - Copy** command or [📋] or [Ctrl] **C**.

*The selected item(s) are placed in the Office Clipboard and are represented by icons on the **Clipboard** toolbar.*

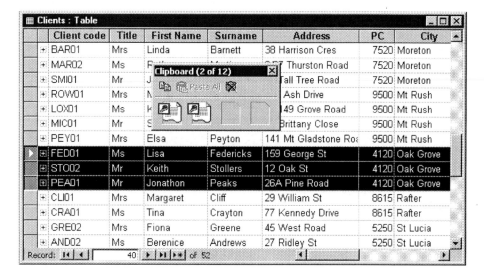

If you point to an icon, a ScreenTip appears showing the first 50 characters of the cut or copied item.

- When you wish to paste an item:

  - click the spot where you wish to paste it. If you are pasting it into a table, query or form in Datasheet view, select the first blank row by clicking the corresponding row selector. If you wish to paste it into another application besides Microsoft Access 2000, go to that application.

  - in the **Clipboard** toolbar, click the icon that corresponds to the item you wish to paste. If the **Clipboard** toolbar is docked, click the **Items** button to see the palette of icons.

- Close the **Clipboard** toolbar by clicking the ⊠ button or by deactivating the **Clipboard** option in the **View - Toolbars** menu.

The Office Clipboard can contain up to 12 items. If you move/copy more than 12 items, a message appears, asking if you want to delete the first item copied.

The Office Clipboard can be used in all Microsoft Office applications. If the Clipboard toolbar is active in Access while another Office application is open, the toolbar will also appear in that application, containing the previously cut/copied items.

Even when you place several items into the Office Clipboard, the last of these items is always copied into the Windows clipboard as well.

The 🔲 Paste All *button on the **Clipboard** toolbar pastes all the items contained in the Office Clipboard. In Microsoft Access, this button is only available when you are working in a data access page.*

The Office Clipboard is emptied automatically when you close all Microsoft Office applications. To empty the Office Clipboard manually, click the 🔲 *tool button on the **Clipboard** toolbar.*

▪ Creating a hyperlink

Creating a hyperlink to an existing file or Web page in a Hyperlink type field

▪ If the hyperlink is to be inserted in a table or query, open the table or query in Datasheet view.
If the hyperlink is to be inserted in a form, open that form in Form view.

▪ Go to the text box of the Hyperlink type field.

▪ **Insert - Hyperlink** or 🔲 or ⌐Ctrl⌐ **K**

▪ Click the **Existing File or Web Page** shortcut on the **Link to** bar.

▪ Fill in the **Type the file or Web page name** box by entering the name of the document to which the link will refer, or click the **File** button to select it. Otherwise, select one of the links that has been used previously from the **Or select from list** box.

*The contents of the **Or select from list** box vary depending on the shortcut chosen. The **Recent Files** shortcut shows the list of the most recently used files, the **Browsed Pages** shortcut shows the list of browsed Web pages and the **Inserted Links** shortcut shows a list of the links most recently added to the links file.*

* If necessary, modify the hyperlink's text in the **Text to display** text box.

* If required, click the **ScreenTip** button and enter the text that should appear when you point to the link. If you do not enter your own text, Access will show the hyperlink's address as the **ScreenTip**.

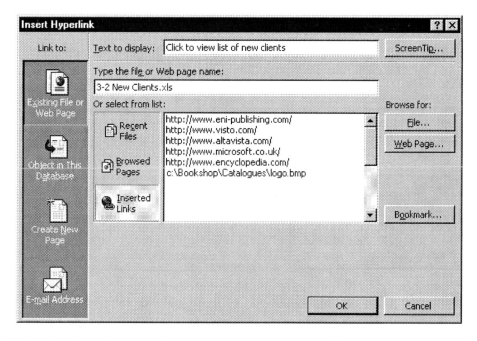

* Use the **Bookmark** button if you wish to select a named location to assign to the hyperlink.

* Click **OK**.

*If no text has been entered in the **Text to display** box in the **Insert Hyperlink** dialog box, the hyperlink text will show the path to the linked document or Web page. When you point to the link (without clicking), the pointer takes the shape of a hand.*

※ To activate the hyperlink, simply click it.

*The linked document appears on the screen along with the **Web** toolbar.*

※ Click the ⬅ tool button to return to the form, table or query window.

Creating a hyperlink towards an object in the current database in a Hyperlink type field

※ If the hyperlink is to be inserted in a table or query, open the table or query in Datasheet view.
If the hyperlink is to be inserted in a form, open that form in Form view.

※ Go to the text box of the Hyperlink type field in the record concerned.

※ **Insert - Hyperlink** or 🖼 or Ctrl **K**

※ Click the **Object in This Database** shortcut on the **Link to** bar.

※ In the list, select the database object to which you wish to establish a link (click the + button on the type of object concerned to see the list of objects it contains).

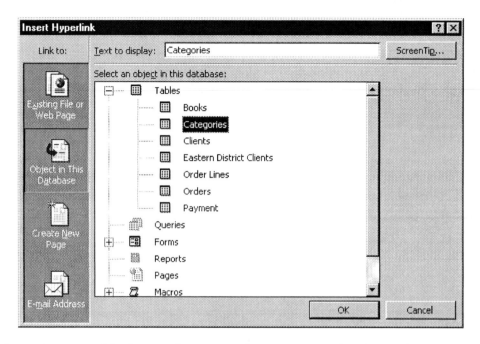

* If necessary, modify the text that you wish to assign to the hyperlink in the **Text to display** box.

* If required, click the **ScreenTip** button and enter the text that should appear when you point to the link. If you do not enter your own text, Access will show the hyperlink's address as the **ScreenTip**.

* Click **OK**.

  *If no text has been entered in the **Text to display** box in the **Insert Hyperlink** dialog box, the hyperlink text will show the name of the database object.*

* To activate the hyperlink, simply click it.

  The database object appears on the screen.

* Click the ⇐ tool button to return to the form, table or query window.

Creating a hyperlink in a form

* Open the form in Design view.

* **Insert - Hyperlink** or 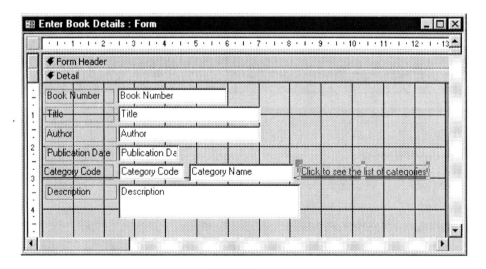 or `Ctrl` **K**

* Click either the **File or Existing Web Page** or **Object in This Database** shortcut, depending on whether you want to create a link to a file, existing Web page or a database object.

* Select the file, Web page or database object to which you wish to make the link.

* Click **OK**.

   *If no text has been entered in the **Text to display** box in the **Insert Hyperlink** dialog box, the hyperlink text will show the file path to the linked file or Web page, or the name of the database object.*

* If required, move the hyperlink within the form window until it is in a satisfactory position.

```
Enter Book Details : Form                                    _ □ ×
  · I · 1 · I · 2 · I · 3 · I · 4 · I · 5 · I · 6 · I · 7 · I · 8 · I · 9 · I · 10 · I · 11 · I · 12 · I · 13

  ◆ Form Header
  ◆ Detail

  Book Number      Book Number
  Title            Title
  Author           Author
  Publication Date  Publication Da
  Category Code    Category Code  Category Name     Click to see the list of categories
  Description      Description
```

* To activate the hyperlink, click the ⊞ ▼ tool button to show the form in Form view then click the hyperlink.

   The database object, document or Web page appears on the screen.

■ Click the ⬅ tool button to show the form window again.

🏛3 ▪ Importing data from another application into a new table

■ Display the database window into which you wish to import the data.

■ **File - Get External Data - Import**

■ Select in the **Files of type** box the type of file containing the data to be imported. To import data from a Microsoft Excel file, select the **Microsoft Excel (*.xls)** option and to import data from a text file, select **Text Files (*.txt;*.csv;*.tab; *.asc)**.

■ Choose the drive then the folder in which the data you are going to import is stored.

■ Click the file concerned then the **Import** button or simply double-click the name of the file you are importing.

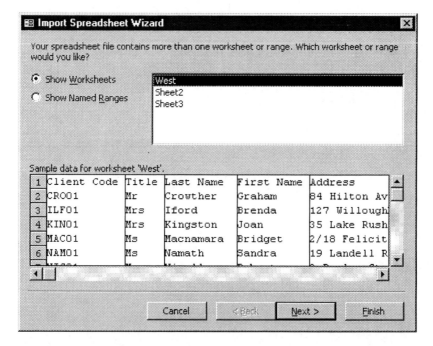

*The first screen of the **Import Wizard** appears. The contents of this window vary depending on the type of data being imported: **Text** or **Spreadsheet**. In the example above, the imported data come from a Microsoft Excel document.*

※ If you are importing data in text format, the wizard informs you whether the text file data are **Delimited** (separated by tabs or commas) or **Fixed Width** (separated by spaces): leave the selected option active. If you are importing data from an Excel document which contains several worksheets or named ranges, activate the **Show Worksheets** option and select the worksheet containing the required data or activate the **Show Named Ranges** option and select the name of the range containing the data you want.

※ Click the **Next** button to go to the next step.

※ If you are importing text file data in a **Delimited** format, select the delimiter that will separate the fields then specify if the **First Row Contains Field Names**; If the data are of **Fixed Width**, define the width of the field following the instructions contained in the window's first frame. If the imported data come from an Excel file, specify if the **First Row Contains Column Headings** then, if required, click the **OK** button on the message that offers to change field names that are not valid as Access field names.

※ Click the **Next** button to go to the next step.

※ Leave the **In a New Table** option active then click the **Next** button.

※ Set the options for each field you are importing in the new table:

- click the corresponding column.

- if required, modify the **Field Name** given.

- in the appropriate list, choose whether or not the filed should be **Indexed** (with or without duplicates).

- if necessary, change the **Data Type** for the selected field.

※ If the chosen field should not be imported into the new table, activate the **Do not import field (Skip)** option.

※ Click the **Next** button to go to the next step.

- If you need to define a primary key for the new table, activate the first option if you want Access to add one for you or the second option if you wish to choose it yourself from the drop-down list to the right of the option. If you do not want to set any primary key for the new table, activate the **No primary key** option.

- Click **Next** then enter the name of the table to which the data should be imported in the **Import to Table** text box and finally click the **Finish** button.

- Click **OK** to close the message telling you that the importation is complete.

4 • Finding data within records

Finding an item of data

- If you wish to search in a table or query, open that table or query in Datasheet view.
  If you wish to search in a form, open the form in Form view.

- Click one of the field values concerned if you wish to search only in that field.

- **Edit - Find** or 🔍 or Ctrl F

- Give the text you are looking for in the **Find What** text box.

- If required, click the **More** button to set further options for the search.

- In the **Search** list box, indicate in which direction Access should search.

- Use the **Match** list box to indicate if the value you are looking for corresponds to an entire field value (**Whole Field**) or only part of the field (**Any Part of Field** or **Start of Field**).

- Activate the **Match Case** option if Access should search for the text with exactly the same combination of upper and lower case letters.

- Activate the **Search Fields As Formatted** option if you want Access to look for the data as they are displayed in the table (with the associated format) and not as they are stored (for example, in Yes/No fields, Access may display the text Yes but the value stored for that field is actually 1).

* In the **Look In** list, select the name of the current field if you only wish to search in that field or select the name of the current datasheet or form if you wish to search in all the fields.

* Click the **Find Next** button to start the search.

   Access highlights the first occurrence of the text it finds. The dialog box may be obstructing the highlighted text; if this is the case, drag it out of the way by its title bar.

* Click the **Find Next** button to look for the next occurrence of the text.

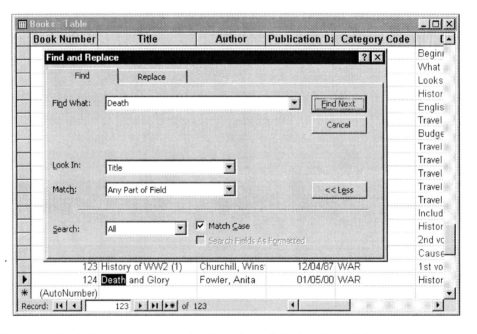

* When you find the text you were looking for, click the **Cancel** button.

* If Access finishes its search and does not find the specified data, a message appears: click **OK**. Close the **Find and Replace** dialog box by clicking its ⊠ button.

   You can use the Shift F4 *shortcut key to continue the last search made without having to open the **Find and Replace** dialog box again.*

Finding data with wildcards

▪ In the **Find and Replace** dialog box, enter the text you are looking for in the **Find What** text box, inserting wildcards characters (such as *, ? or #) as needed, following the guidelines below:

- the * character is used to represent a string of characters of variable length,

- the ? character is used to represent a single character,

- the # character replaces a single number,

- square brackets ([ ]) are used to give a choice of several characters,

- the [!] character excludes the characters in the brackets from the search.

▪ For example:

The search text	will find	but will not find
s*w	sew, sinew, somehow	jigsaw
??aw	thaw	law, straw
## dogs	10 dogs	my dogs
WAL[LK]ER	WALKER, WALLER	WALTER
WAL[!LK]ER	WALTER	WALKER, WALLER

▪ If required, set the other search options (**Match**, **Search** etc) then start the search.

The **Find - Replace** command or ⌨Ctrl **H** can be used to replace one item of data by another, using the same search principles.

Below you can see **Practice Exercise** 3.2. This exercise is made up of 4 steps. If you do not know how to complete one of the steps, go back to the lesson to refer to the corresponding title. When you have finished, check your work by reading the **Solution** on the next page.

All the steps in this exercise are likely to be tested during the exam.

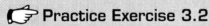

☞ Practice Exercise 3.2

*To work through exercise 3.2, open the **3-2 BookBase.mdb** database located in the **MOUS Access 2000** folder.*

1. Complete the **Eastern District Clients** table by pasting into it the records concerning clients from **Eastport** and **Oak Grove** that are in the **Clients** table. Use the **Office Clipboard** to do this. Finish by closing the **Clipboard** toolbar then the **Eastern District Clients** table.

2. In the **Enter Book Details** form, insert a hyperlink to the **Categories** table. Assign the text **Click to see the list of categories** to the hyperlink and position it to the right of the **Category Name** text box. Next, activate the hyperlink then return to the **Enter Book Details** form window. To finish, save and close the **Enter Book Details** form and close the **Categories** table.

3. Into a new table that you will call **Western District Clients**, import the data from the **West** worksheet, which is in the **3-2 New Clients.xls** workbook, in the **MOUS Access 2000** folder. While importing, make sure that:
   - you use the column headings as field names,
   - you index the **Client Code** field (without duplicates),
   - you change the **Address** field to **Street Address**,
   - you define the **Client Code** field as the primary key.

Next, open the **Western District Clients** table in Datasheet view to view its contents then close it.

4. Search the **Title** column of the **Books** table for the word **Death**, respecting the combination of upper case and lowercase letters. You can stop the search when you reach the title called **Death and Glory** then close the **Books** table.

If you want to put what you have learned into practice in a real document you can work on summary exercise 3 for the MANAGING DATA section that can be found at the end of this book.

It is often possible to perform a task in several different ways, but here only the most efficient solution is presented. You can go back to the lesson if you wish to see the other techniques that can be used.

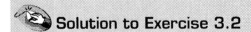

Solution to Exercise 3.2

1. To complete the Eastern District Clients table by pasting into it the records concerning clients from Eastport and Oak Grove that are in the Clients table, start by clicking **Tables** in the objects bar. Double-click the **Clients** table icon to open it in Datasheet view.

   Display the **Clipboard** toolbar with the **View - Toolbars - Clipboard** command.

   To copy the records concerning clients from **Eastport**, click the row selector for the first record whose City field reads **Eastport** (record 9). Drag the mouse downwards until it reaches the last record for **Eastport** (record 13). Next, click the [icon] tool button on the **Clipboard** toolbar.

   To copy the records concerning clients from **Oak Grove**, click the row selector for the first record whose City field reads **Oak Grove** (record 40). Drag the mouse downwards until it reaches the last record for **Oak Grove** (record 42) then click the [icon] tool button on the **Clipboard** toolbar.

   Close the Clients table with the **File - Close** command then open the **Eastern District Clients** table by double-clicking its icon.

   To add the records concerning **Eastport** into the Eastern District Clients table, click the row selector of the first empty row at the end of the table then click the first icon on the **Clipboard** toolbar. Next, click **Yes** on the message that tells you you are about to paste 5 records into the table.

To add the records concerning **Oak Grove** into the Eastern District Clients table, click the row selector of the first empty row at the end of the table then click the second icon on the **Clipboard** toolbar. Next, click **Yes** on the message that tells you you are about to paste 3 records into the table.

To close the **Clipboard** toolbar, click the ☒ button in its top right corner. To close the **Eastern District Clients** table, activate the **File - Close** command.

2. To insert a hyperlink into the Enter Book Details form that links it to the Categories table, start by clicking **Forms** on the objects bar. Select the **Enter Book Details** form by clicking its name then click the [Design] button to open it

Click the [tool] tool button then click the **Object in This Database** shortcut. Click the **+** sign to the left of **Tables** to see the list of tables then click the **Categories** table. Select the text that is in the **Text to display** box and type **Click to see the list of categories** then click **OK**.

To position the hyperlink to the right of the Category Name text box, point to the hyperlink until the pointer becomes a hand then drag the link to the right of the **Category Name** text box.

To activate the hyperlink, click the [tool] tool button to show the form in Form view then click the hyperlink.

To return to the Enter Book Details form window, click the [tool] tool button.

To save then close the Enter Book Details form, click the [tool] tool button then use the **File - Close** command.

To close the Categories table, use the **File - Close** command.

3. To import into a new table the data from the West worksheet (in the 3-2 New Clients.xls workbook located in the MOUS Access 2000 folder), activate the **File - Get External Data - Import** command.

Open the **Files of type** drop-down list and choose the **Microsoft Excel (*.xls)** option. Open the **Look in** list then select the drive in which you installed the documents from the CD-ROM supplied with this book. Double-click the **MOUS Access 2000** folder then double-click the **3-2 New Clients.xls** file.

Check that the **West** sheet is selected then click the **Next** button. Activate the **First Row Contains Column Headings** option then click **Next**. Leave the **In a New Table** option active and click **Next**.

To index the Client Code field, without allowing duplicates, click the **Client Code** column, open the **Indexed** drop-down list and click the **Yes (No Duplicates)** option.

To change the Address field to Street Address, click the **Address** column, select the contents of the **Field Name** box and enter **Street Address**.

Click the **Next** button to go to the next step.

To set the Client Code field as the primary key, activate the **Choose my own primary key** option then if necessary open the drop-down list to select the **Client Code** field.

Click the **Next** button, enter the text **Western District Clients** in the **Import to Table** text box then click the **Finish** button. Click **OK** on the message telling you that the importation is finished.

To open the Western District Clients table to view its contents, click **Tables** in the objects bar (if necessary) then double-click the **Western District Clients** icon. To close the table, use the **File - Close** command.

4. To look for the word Death in the Title column of the Books table, click **Tables** in the objects bar then double-click the **Books** table icon. Click the first value in the **Title** field then use the **Edit - Find** command.

Enter the word **Death** in the **Find What** text box. Open the **Match** drop-down list and select the **Any Part of Field** option. Click the **More** button then, to ensure the upper and lower case letters are matched, tick the **Match Case** option. Click the **Find Next** button twice until the **Death and Glory** title appears then close the **Find and Replace** dialog box by clicking its ✖ button.

To close the **Books** table, activate the **File - Close** command.

MANAGING DATA
Exercise 3.2: Data

MANAGING DATA
Lesson 3.3: Printing data

1 ▪ Using the print preview

* Click the name of the table, query, form or report of which you wish to see a preview before printing.

* **File - Print Preview** or

  The data appear on the screen as they will appear on the printed page. When the mouse pointer is positioned on the page, it takes the shape of a magnifying glass.

* To increase the magnification level of the preview, position the pointer over the area you want to zoom and click. To reduce the zoom, click the page.

* To select another zoom value, open the corresponding list on the **Print Preview** toolbar and click the required zoom level.

* To scroll through the pages, use the buttons located in the lower left corner of the window. To go to a particular page, double-click the active page number, type the number of the page you want, then enter.

* To see several pages of the preview at once, click the tool button then drag to select the number of pages you wish to see and the layout of that display; for example, the tool button shows two pages of the preview at a time.

* To return to a one page display, click the tool button.

* To start printing, click the tool button.

* To close the print preview, click the **Close** button on the **Print Preview** toolbar or press the Esc key.

> *The print preview can also be displayed from Datasheet view in a table or query, from Form view in a form or from Design view in a report.*

2 ▪ Printing a table, query or form

▪ In the database window, select the name of the table, query or form that you wish to print and click the [⊞ Open] button.

▪ If necessary, change the layout until you have the required presentation.

▪ To set the printing margins, use the **File - Page Setup** command and click the **Margins** tab.

▪ For a table or query, activate or deactivate the **Print Headings** option depending on whether or not you wish to print the column headings.
For a form or report, activate the **Print Data Only** option if you do not wish to print the labels, control outlines, gridlines or pictures.

▪ To set the printing orientation, use the **Portrait** or **Landscape** options under the **Page** tab.

▪ Click **OK** to close the **Page Setup** dialog box.

▪ **File - Print** or [Ctrl] **P**

▪ To print all the records in the table, query or form, make sure the **All** option is active.

▪ To print only certain pages, click the **From** text box and type the number of the first page you want to print, then click the **To** box and enter the last page you wish to print.

▪ If you selected some records before printing, click the **Selected Record(s)** option to print just that selection.

▪ To print several copies, enter the required **Number of Copies** in the corresponding text box (in the **Copies** frame). If necessary, activate the **Collate** option to print one copy of the whole document (or selection) before starting on the next. For example, pages 1, 2 and 3 are printed twice in succession, instead of printing two copies of page 1, two copies of 2, and two copies of 3.

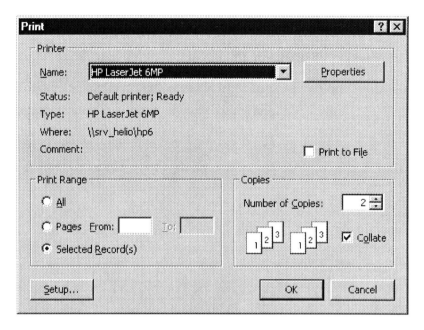

* Click the **OK** button.

 You can also print a table, query or form after having simply selected its name in the database window. In this case you cannot select the records you wish to print.

By default, Access prints a header containing the name of the table, query or form, the day's date and a footer with the page number.

The printing configuration options are saved with a report or with a form. This is not the case when you change these settings to print a datasheet.

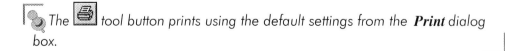 *The* 🖶 *tool button prints using the default settings from the **Print** dialog box.*

Below you can see **Practice Exercise** 3.3. This exercise is made up of 2 steps. If you do not know how to complete one of the steps, go back to the lesson to refer to the corresponding title. When you have finished, check your work by reading the **Solution** on the next page.

Steps that are likely to be tested in the exam are marked with a ▦ symbol. It is however recommended that you follow the whole exercise in order to gain a complete understanding of the lesson.

☞ Practice Exercise 3.3

To work through exercise 3.3, open the ***3-3 BookBase.mdb*** database located in the ***MOUS Access 2000*** folder.

1. Show a print preview for the **Clients** table then make the following changes:
   - show four pages of the preview at a time: 2 pages down and two pages across.
   - show the preview as a single page again.
   - zoom in on the column headings that can be seen in the preview.
   - close the print preview window.

▦ 2. Print two copies of records **35** to **63** (books in the CRI category) in the **Books** table. Print two complete copies rather than page by page. To finish, close the **Books** table.

If you want to put what you have learned into practice in a real document you can work on summary exercise 3 for the MANAGING DATA section that can be found at the end of this book.

It is often possible to perform a task in several different ways, but here only the most efficient solution is presented. You can go back to the lesson if you wish to see the other techniques that can be used.

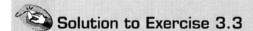

Solution to Exercise 3.3

1. To show the print preview for the Clients table, click **Tables** in the objects bar, select the **Clients** table then activate the **File - Print Preview** command.

   To show four pages of the document in the preview (2 pages across and 2 pages down), click the 🖼 tool button then drag to select the 2 x 2 pages option.

   To show the preview as a single page again, click the 🖼 tool button.

   To magnify the column headings seen in the preview, position the pointer at the top of the page, over the column headings and click.

   To close the print preview window, click the **Close** button on the **Print Preview** toolbar.

2. To print two copies of records 35 to 63 in the Books table, click **Tables** in the objects bar then double-click the **Books** table icon. Click the row selector on record **35** then drag to spread the selection to record **63**. Now, activate the **File - Print** command.
   Activate the **Selected Record(s)** option and enter **2** in the **Number of Copies** text box. Tick the **Collate** option to print two distinct copies. Start printing by clicking the **OK** button.

   To close the **Books** table, choose **File - Close**.

CREATING FORMS AND REPORTS
Lesson 4.1: Forms

CREATING FORMS AND REPORTS
Lesson 4.1: Forms

1 ▪ Creating an AutoForm

This technique creates a form with a predefined presentation.

▪ Click **Forms** on the objects bar then click the 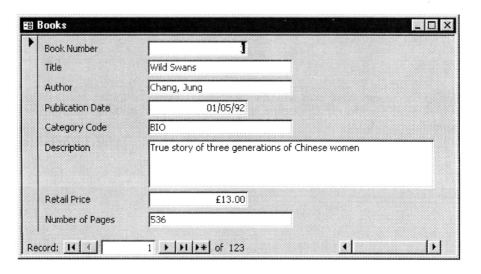 **New** button on the database window toolbar.

▪ Click the type of presentation you want your AutoForm to have: **AutoForm: Columnar, AutoForm: Tabular** or **AutoForm: Datasheet**.

▪ Open the drop-down list box and choose the table or query for which you wish to create an AutoForm.

▪ Click **OK**.

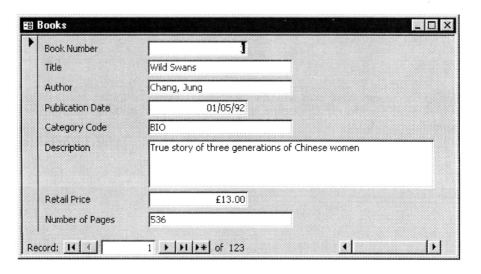

▣ Books	_ ▢ ✕
▶ Book Number	
Title	Wild Swans
Author	Chang, Jung
Publication Date	01/05/92
Category Code	BIO
Description	True story of three generations of Chinese women
Retail Price	£13.00
Number of Pages	536

Record: ◄◄ ◄ | 1 | ► ►► ►✱ of 123

The AutoForm appears on the screen, ready for use. The example above shows a columnar style of form: the fields are placed one beneath the other. Only one record at a time can be seen.

The buttons in the bottom left corner of the window can be used, as in a datasheet, to move through the various records.

* If required, save the form. To do this, use the **File - Save** command, or 🖫 or
 Ctrl **S**, enter the **Form Name** in the corresponding text box and click **OK**.

> You can use this form as it is to add, delete or modify records, or you can
> go into its design and customise it or simply use it and delete it.

2 ▪ Creating a form with a wizard

*A form is used to work with the records from a table by means of a special data
entry window. If you wish to use the form to work only with certain records, you
should base it on a query. The table or query from which a form is created is
known as its **source**.*

* There are three techniques you can use to create a form with a wizard:

 - click **Forms** in the objects bar then click the [New] button on the database
 window,

 - click **Forms** on the objects bar then click the **Create form by using wizard**
 shortcut,

 - select the table or query for which you want to create a form, open the drop-
 down list on the **New Object** tool button, then click the **Form** option (or
 select the table or query and use the **Insert - Form** command).

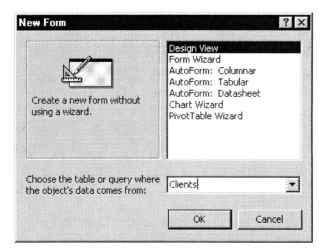

This dialog box does not appear if you choose the **Create form by using wizard** *shortcut.*

* Click the **Form Wizard** option.

* If necessary, open the drop-down list and select the table or query for which you want to create a form.

* Click **OK**.

* Specify which fields from the table should be inserted in the form.

  - select each field you want to insert from the **Available Fields** list then click the
    > button.

  - to insert all the fields from the list, click the >> button.

  - to remove a field you have selected, click it in the **Selected Fields** list then click the < button.

  - to remove all the fields, click the << button.

  You can also insert a field by double-clicking it.

* Click **Next** to go to the next step.

* Choose the type of layout you want the fields in the form to have. A click on each option shows a preview of its effects.

* Click **Next**.

- Choose a style for your form. A click on each option shows a preview of its effects.

- Click **Next**.

- Give the text that should appear on the form's title bar.

  The form will also be saved under this title.

- Choose the first option if you wish to view the records immediately through the created form (in Form view) or the second of you wish to see the form's structure or design (Design view).

- Activate the **Display Help on working with the form?** option if you wish to read a help text on how to use a form.

- Click the **Finish** button.

  The form appears on the screen, ready to be used. The buttons in the bottom left corner of the window can be used, as in a datasheet, to move through the various records.

- To show a form in Design view in order to modify its design, click the ⬚ tool button on the **Form View** toolbar.

  *You can use the **View** button (⬚) to take you back to Form view.*

  In addition to the form window, three other windows may be visible on the screen: the property sheet, the field list and the toolbox. You can open these windows manually by clicking the corresponding tool buttons:

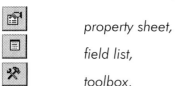

property sheet,

field list,

toolbox.

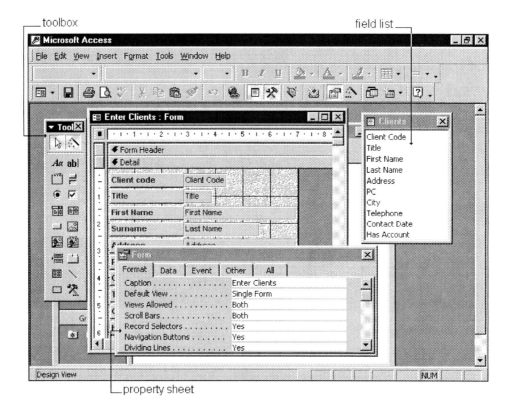

By default, a form is made up of three sections:

*- the **Form Header**,*

*- the **Detail** section,*

*- the **Form Footer**.*

*Each element inserted in a form is called a **control**. For example, the form's title and the various labels shown are all controls.*

*When you insert a field into a form, Access adds two controls: a **field label** which contains a text that you can modify or delete (initially the name of the field) and a **text box** that displays the field value in Form view (this is vital for managing field data in the form).*

There are three types of control available:

- *unbound controls* *which show information that is independent from the source table or query (for example a text you have entered into the form or a drawing object such as a rectangle or line),*

- *bound controls* *which are linked to a field in the source table/query and which generally display the corresponding field value,*

- *calculated controls* *which show data calculated from one or more field values using an expression that you create. For example, in a Products form, a Retail Price control will show a value calculated from the article's price plus sales tax.*

3 ▪ Setting a form's tab order

This technique sets the *tab order* *of a form. This is the order in which fields are accessed when you press the* ⬚ *or* ⬚ *key while using the form.*

▪ Click **Forms** in the objects bar, select the form whose tab order you wish to modify then click the ⬚ Design button.

▪ **View - Tab Order**

» In the **Section** frame, select the option corresponding to the appropriate section of the form.

» Check the order in which the fields will be accessed, defined from top to bottom and from left to right. To move a field within the **Custom Order** list, select the field by clicking its field selector. Then drag the field until the black horizontal line that appears is placed in the required position.

*To set a tab order that follows how the fields are physically placed on the form, from left to right and from top to bottom, click the **Auto Order** button.*

» Click **OK**.

» If necessary, click the [icon] tool button to go to Form view.

» Click the [icon] tool button to save your changes then, if required, close the form with the **File - Close** command.

4 ▪ Associating a table with a form

You can use this technique to work with data from one table using a form that was originally created for another table (the two tables must have a similar structure).

» Click **Forms** in the objects bar, select the name of the form and click the [icon] Design button.

» Show the form's property sheet by clicking the [icon] tool button then click the square at the intersection of the horizontal and vertical rulers ([icon]).

*The form's properties appear in a separate window; they are grouped by type and each type has its own page in the window which you can see by clicking the appropriate tab. The **All** page lists all the properties whatever their type.*

» Click the **Data** tab then in the **Record Source** box, select the table that you wish to associate with the form.

∗ Click the **Format** tab then in the **Caption** text box modify (if you wish) the title that will be seen on the window's title bar when in Form view.

∗ Save the changes made to the form by clicking the ⊞ tool button then if required close the form with **File - Close**

5 ∗ Inserting a subform

Subforms are used to display simultaneously the data from two tables that are linked by a "one-to-many" relationship. The main form represents the "one" side of the relationship and the subform the "many" side. The subform can appear as a datasheet or as a classic form. In the example below, the subform shows the books that have been ordered by each client.

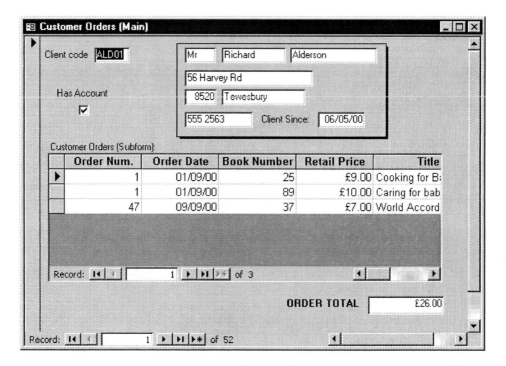

∗ Create the subform as any other form and show it in Design view.

If the subform needs to include values from fields in several tables, create a query regrouping those fields then make that query the source of the subform.

- Display the subform's property sheet. To do this, click the square at the intersection of the horizontal and vertical rulers (⬚) then click the 🖳 tool button.

- Click the **Format** tab, open the list on the **Views Allowed** property and choose which type of display you wish to allow for the subform:

Form	The subform will be displayed like any other form (one record at a time).
Datasheet	The subform will be displayed as a datasheet.
Both	The subform can be displayed in either of these views.

- In the **Default View** property, select the view you wish to set as the default when you open the subform. **Continuous Forms** uses a form display but which will show several records at once, as far as the form's height allows.

- Click the **Data** tab then use the following properties to determine how you wish to use the form:

Allow Filters	do you want to use the form to filter records?
Allow Edits	do you want to use the form to modify records?
Allow Deletions	do you want to use the form to delete records?
Allow Additions	do you want to use the form to add new records?
Data Entry	activate this property if the form will be used solely for adding new records.

- Click the 🖫 tool button to save the subform then close it with the **File - Close** command.

- Open the main form in **Design** view (🖾▾).

- Simultaneously display the form and database windows using the **Window - Tile Horizontally** or **Tile Vertically** command.

» Drag the subform's icon from the database window to the **Detail** section in the main form window.

*Access inserts a control with the same name as the subform. The **Subform** can be seen inside that control.*

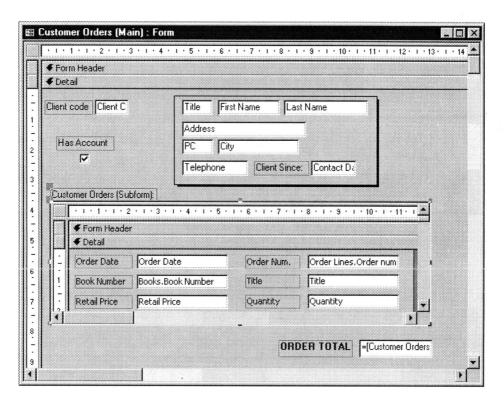

» Use the **Window - Cascade** command to overlap the two windows then if necessary, resize the main form window.

» If necessary, click the subform (selection handles represented by black squares appear around the control) then show its property sheet by clicking the ▤ tool button.

※ Click the **Data** tab then check the **Link Child Fields** and **Link Master Fields** properties. The child field is the linking field in the subform and the master field is the linking field in the main form.

*Access sets these two elements automatically when a relationship exists between the two tables, or failing that, if the two tables have a field with the same name and identical data. However, if the main form is based on a query, you have to define the **Link Child Fields** and **Link Master Fields** properties yourself. If one of the two forms is based on a query, the query must contain the linking field (the child field in the subform or the master field in the main form) although that field need not necessarily be visible in the form.*

※ If necessary, move the subform control and/or change its size.

※ Click the 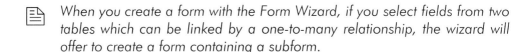 tool button to view the result.

※ In Form view, if you wish to see the subform as a datasheet or as a form, click the subform and choose **View - Subform Datasheet**.

*This option is only available if you chose the **Both** option for the **Views Allowed** property (on the **Format** page).*

※ Use the buttons in the bottom left corner of the subform to scroll through the records.

※ Click the ☐ tool button to save the form then if required, close it with **File - Close**.

📄 *When you create a form with the Form Wizard, if you select fields from two tables which can be linked by a one-to-many relationship, the wizard will offer to create a form containing a subform.*

Below you can see **Practice Exercise** 4.1. This exercise is made up of 5 steps. If you do not know how to complete one of the steps, go back to the lesson to refer to the corresponding title. When you have finished, check your work by reading the **Solution** on the next page.

Steps that are likely to be tested in the exam are marked with a ▥ symbol. It is however recommended that you follow the whole exercise in order to gain a complete understanding of the lesson.

☞ Practice Exercise 4.1

To work through exercise 4-1, you should open the **4-1 BookBase.mdb** database located in the **MOUS Access 2000** folder.

1. Create an AutoForm with a columnar layout based on the **Books** table. Save this form (as **Enter Books**) then close it.

▥ 2. Create a form using the wizard, based on the **Clients** table:
   - you must add all the fields from the Clients table to the form,
   - the form should be presented in a column style
   - apply a **Stone** style to the form,
   - the text **Enter Clients** should appear in the title bar.
   To finish, close this form.

3. Change the tab order of the **Enter Books** form so the fields are accessed in this order: Book Number, Category Code, Title, Author, Publication Date, Description, Number of Pages and Retail Price. Save then close the **Enter Books** form.

4. Associate the **Eastern District Clients** table with the **Enter Clients** form. The text **Enter Eastern District Clients** should appear on the title bar of this form. Close the property sheet then save and close the form.

5. Insert the **Customer Orders (Subform)** form as a subform into the **Customer Orders (Main)** main form. It should be positioned 4 cm (or 1¾ in) from the top of the **Detail** section, as shown on the screen below:

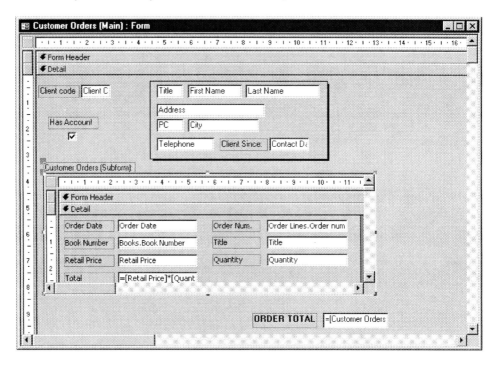

Apply a **Datasheet** view as the default view for the subform; do not allow data to be filtered, modified, deleted or added by means of this subform.

Save the main form then display it in Form view and scroll through the first three records. Finish by closing the main form.

If you want to put what you have learned into practice in a real document you can work on summary exercise 4 for the CREATING FORMS AND REPORTS section that can be found at the end of this book.

It is often possible to perform a task in several different ways, but here only the most efficient solution is presented. You can go back to the lesson if you wish to see the other techniques that can be used.

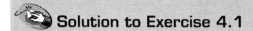

Solution to Exercise 4.1

1. To create an AutoForm with a columnar layout whose source should be the Books table, click **Forms** in the objects bar then click the [New] button. Click the **AutoForm: Columnar** option, open the drop-down list and select the **Books** table then click **OK**.

   To save the form under the name Enter Books, click the [tool] tool button, enter **Enter Books** in the text box and click **OK**.

   To close the Enter Books form, use the **File - Close** command.

2. To create a form with a wizard, with the Clients table as the form's source, click **Forms** in the objects bar then click the [New] button.

   Click the **Form Wizard** option then open the drop-down list and select the **Clients** table. Click **OK**. Add all the fields from the Clients table into the form by clicking the [>>] button then click **Next**. Leave the **Columnar** option active then click **Next**. Select the form style called **Stone** then click **Next** again. Enter the text **Enter Clients** in the text box then click the **Finish** button.

   To close the form, use **File - Close**.

3. To set the field tab order as described in step 3, click **Forms** on the objects bar, select the **Enter Books** form and click the [Design] button. Activate the **View - Tab Order** command and leave the **Detail** option active.

To move the Category Code field before the Title field, click the row selector for the **Category Code** field. Next, drag the row selector for the **Category Code** field; a black horizontal line appears as you drag. Place this line above the **Title** field.

To move the Number of Pages field before the Retail Price field, click the row selector of the **Number of Pages** field. Drag the row selector for the **Number of Pages** field until the horizontal line that appears is above the **Retail Price** field. Click **OK**.

To save and close the Enter Books form, click the 🖫 tool then use the **File - Close** command.

4. To associate the Eastern District Clients table with the Enter Clients form, click **Forms** on the objects bar, select the **Enter Clients** form then click the ⬛ Design button.

Click the 🖼 tool button then click the intersection of the horizontal and vertical rulers to show the form's properties. Click the **Data** tab then in the **Record Source** property choose **Eastern District Clients**. Click the **Format** tab and in the **Caption** property, enter **Enter Eastern District Clients**.

To close the property sheet, click the ❎ button on its window.

To save then close the Enter Clients form, click the 🖫 tool then activate the **File - Close** command.

5. Before inserting the Customer Orders (Subform) form into the Customer Orders (Main) form, you should start by modifying some of the subform's properties. To do this, click **Forms** in the objects bar then select the **Customer Orders (Subform)** form and click the ⬛ Design button. Next, click the 🖼 tool button then the square at the intersection of the horizontal and vertical rulers to see the subform's properties.

To apply Datasheet view as the allowed view for the subform, click the **Format** tab then select the **Datasheet** option in the **Views Allowed** and **Default View** properties.

To ensure no data is filtered, modified, deleted or added, click the **Data** tab then select the **No** option for these properties: **Allow Filters**, **Allow Edits**, **Allow Deletions** and **Allow Additions**.

Click the ⊞ tool button to save the subform then use **File - Close**.

Select the **Customer Orders (Main)** form then click the ⛏ Design button to see its design. Use the **Window - Tile Vertically** command to display the form window and the database window simultaneously. Click the **Customer Orders (Subform)** icon in the database window then drag this icon over to the main form window, positioning it as shown in part 5 of the practice exercice.

To save the changes made to the main form, click the ⊞ tool button.

Next, click the ▣ tool button to display the form in Form view. To maximise the form on the screen, click the ▢ button on its title bar. Scroll through the records with the ▶ button that appears at the base of the window then close the main form by using **File - Close**.

CREATING FORMS AND REPORTS
Exercise 4.1: Forms

CREATING FORMS AND REPORTS
Lesson 4.2: Reports

📖 1 ▪ Creating a report with a wizard

A report is used to print the information from a table or query with a predefined presentation. A report can also contain various calculations.

▪ You can use one of three techniques to create a new report with a wizard:

- click **Reports** on the objects bar then click the 🖥 New button on the database window,

- click **Reports** on the objects bar then click the **Create report by using wizard** shortcut.

▪ Select the table or query on which you want to base your report, open the list on the **New Object** tool button 🔳 ▾ then click the **Report** option (or select the object and use **Insert - Report**).

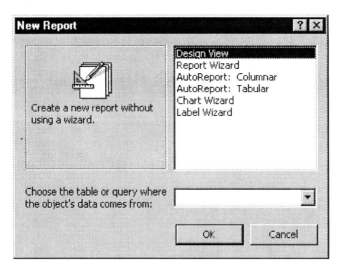

*This dialog box does not appear if you use the **Create report by using wizard** shortcut.*

*The **Design View** option takes you to a blank report in Design view, so you can create the report yourself. The **Chart Wizard** creates a report containing a chart and the **Label Wizard** creates a report for printing labels.*

▪ Click the **Report Wizard** option.

» If necessary, open the drop-down list and choose the table or query for which you wish to create a report.

» If you only wish to print certain records with the report, you should base it on a query. The selected table or query is known as the report's **source**.

» Click **OK**.

» Specify which fields you wish to include in the report:

- select each field you want to insert in the **Available Fields** list and click the ▢ button.

- to insert all the available fields, click the ▢ button.

- to remove a field you have selected, click it in the **Selected Fields** list and click the ▢ button.

- to remove all the selected fields, click ▢.

You can also insert a field by double-clicking its name.

» Click the **Next** button to go to the next step.

» If you wish to group certain records in the report, select the field by which you wish to group then click the ▢ button. You can repeat this action if you wish to add several grouping levels.

» To delete a grouping level, click the corresponding field name in the preview window then click the ▢ button.

» To modify the order of the grouping fields, click the name of the field concerned in the preview window then use the ▢ button to move it up one level or ▢ to move it down one level.

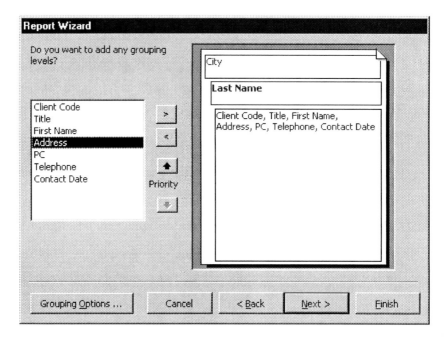

*The **Grouping Options** button can be used to change the options concerning group intervals, namely which values are used to determine each group interval.*

※ Click the **Next** button.

※ Give the sort order that should be used when the records are printed: for each field by which you want to sort, open the first empty list box, select the field then click the ![ascending button] button to sort by ascending order or the ![descending button] button to sort by descending order.

The field in list 1 will be used as the first sort key, the one in list 2 as the second sort key and so on.

※ Click the **Next** button.

※ Specify how the fields should be laid out:

Columnar The fields are laid out one beneath the other, as in any columnar form or report.

Tabular   The fields are laid out one next to the other and the records placed one beneath the other, which gives a table presentation not unlike a datasheet.

Justified   The data from each record appear in a table of equal height and width.

The layouts on offer change when one or more group levels are defined in the report: Stepped, Block, Outline 1, Outline 2 etc. Click each option to see the corresponding example.

⬦ Activate the **Adjust the field width...** option to print each record on a single line.

⬦ Select the required page **Orientation** in the corresponding frame: **Portrait** or **Landscape**.

⬦ Click **Next**.

⬦ Choose the style you want for your report. You can click each option to see a preview of its effects.

⬦ Click **Next**.

⬦ Type the text that should appear in the report's title bar.

This is also the name under which the report will be saved.

⬦ Activate **Preview the report** to see the result or **Modify the report's design** to go into Design view.

⬦ Activate the **Display Help on working with the report?** option if you want to get help with managing the report.

⬦ Click the **Finish** button.

⬦ Scroll through the pages of the preview using the buttons in the bottom left corner of the window.

Like a form, a report is made up of several sections:

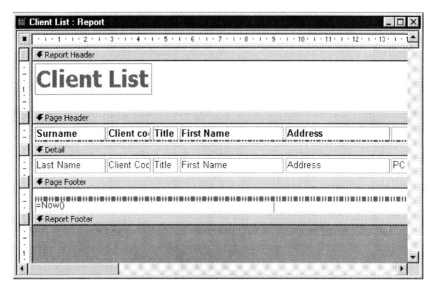

- the **Report Header** contains data that will only print at the start of the first page of the report,

- the **Page Header** contains the data that will print at the start of each page (the column headings for example),

- the **Detail** section contains the data printed for each record (this generally consists of the text boxes for each field),

- the **Page Footer** contains the data that will print at the bottom of each page. You can use the Now() function to obtain the day's date, the Page function to insert automatic page numbering and the Pages function to obtain the total number of pages.

- finally, the **Report Footer** is reserved for data that will appear on the last page of the report, after all the records.

As with a form, several different types of control can be found within a report's design:

- bound controls,

- *unbound controls: these could be for example, the report's title, the column titles, horizontal lines and so on,*

- *calculated controls: examples of calculated controls are controls that display the current date or number the pages.*

 The width of the report should not be greater than that of the paper used for printing (minus the set printing margins).

*You can modify a report's presentation by using the **Format - AutoFormat** command (or*  *) then applying one of the styles offered by the wizard.*

To show the report's properties, double-click the grey area outside of the limits of the report or click the box at the intersection of the horizontal and vertical rulers.

*It is possible to insert the day's date and automatic page numbering using the first two options in the **Insert** menu.*

As with forms, you can create an AutoReport using the 🖫 New *button on the database window.*

2 ▪ Grouping records on a report

▪ Click **Reports** on the objects bar, select the name of the report in which you wish to group records then click the 🔩 Design *button to view its design.*

▪ **View - Sorting and Grouping** or 【≡

In order to print records by group, you must first define a sort order according to the different groups.

※ Set the sort order for the records in the top part of the dialog box. For each field by which you wish to sort, open the first empty list box in the **Field/Expression** column, select the field then select the appropriate **Sort Order** (ascending or descending).

※ For each sort order defined, activate the **Group Header** and **Group Footer** options at the bottom of the dialog box if you wish to group by that field.

Access subsequently creates two new sections (that can be seen on the report in the background) called ***(Name of group) Header*** *and* ***(Name of group) Footer***. *The first is for data printed at the beginning of each new group and the second for data printed at the end of each group.*

※ For each grouping level, specify by what value Access should **Group On** and at what **Group Interval**. The type of grouping made depends on the type of field used.

For a Text type field:

Each Value	Access groups the records where the field values are the same.
Prefix Characters	Access groups records where the first X characters of the field value are identical; X is defined in **Group Interval**.

For a Number, Currency or AutoNumber type field:

Each Value	Access groups the records where the field values are identical.
Interval	Access groups the records according to the **Group Interval** given, beginning at the value 0. For example, if the **Group Interval** option equals 10, Access groups the records whose field value is between 0 and 9 then 10 and 19 and so on.

To group on a Date/Time type field:

You can group by **Year**, by **Qtr** (quarter), by **Month**, by **Week**, by **Day**, by **Hour** or by **Minute**. The **Group Interval** defines how many years, quarters, months etc are counted.

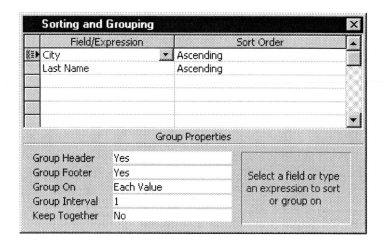

- Using the **Keep Together** option, indicate how Access should manage page breaks within each group:

  No   The group of records can be printed on two different pages.

  Whole group   Access makes a page break before starting to print the next group, if it will not fit into the bottom of the page.

  With first detail The group can be printed over two pages but the group heading will not be printed at the bottom of a page unless it is accompanied by at least one record

- Close the **Sorting and Grouping** window by clicking the ⊠ button or with the 〔≡ tool button on the **Report Design** toolbar.

- Place your required elements in the **Group Header** and **Group Footer** sections.

- Start the print preview and/or begin printing the report.

- Save the report by clicking the 💾 tool button then close it with the **File - Close** command.

Grouping can be based on a calculated field.

You can modify the sorting and grouping orders by changing the contents of the **Sorting and Grouping** *dialog box:*
- *to delete a grouping level, click the corresponding field selector and press* Del *,*
- *to insert a row in order to define a new grouping level, click the row selector before which you wish to insert the row then press the* Insert *key,*
- *to move a row to modify the sorting or grouping order, click its row selector and drag the row into its new position.*

3 ▪ Previewing and printing a report

▪ Click **Reports** in the objects bar then double-click the name of the report you wish to preview and print.

You can see the report in **Print Preview** *view. The data appear on the screen as they would on the printed page. When you position the mouse pointer over the page, it takes the form of a magnifying glass.*

▪ To increase the preview's zoom level, position the pointer over the area you wish to magnify and click. To reduce the zoom level, click the scaled-down page. To select a specific zoom value, open the appropriate list box on the **Print Preview** toolbar then choose the required zoom value.

▪ To scroll through the pages, use the buttons that can be seen in the bottom left corner of the window.

▪ To view several pages of the preview at once, click the 🔲 tool button then drag to choose the button that displays the required number of pages and page layout. For example, the 🔲 tool button displays two preview pages at a time.

▪ To return to a single page preview, click the 🔲 tool button.

- To start printing with the default print settings, click the 🖨 tool button: this will print one copy of all the pages in the report.

- To define the print settings, use the **File - Print** command or ⌨Ctrl **P**.

- To print every page in the preview, check that the **All** option is active. If you wish to print a group of pages, activate the **Pages** option in the **Print Range** frame and in the **From** and **To** boxes, give the numbers of the first and last pages you want to print.

- To print several copies, enter the required **Number of Copies** in the corresponding text box (in the **Copies** frame). If necessary, activate the **Collate** option to print one copy of the whole document (or selection) before starting on the next. For example, pages 1, 2 and 3 are printed twice in succession, instead of printing two copies of page 1, two copies of 2, and two copies of 3.

- Click **OK** to start printing.

- To close the print preview, click the **Close** button on the **Print Preview** toolbar or press the ⌨Esc key.

📄 *When you are working on the report's structure (in Design view), you can preview just a few records using the **View - Layout Preview** command or by choosing the **Layout Preview** option from the **View** tool button 🔍▾ on the toolbar.*

You can also print a report after having selected its name in the database window.

🔍 *If a blank page is produced between each printed page, check that the width of the report is compatible with the width of the paper; if necessary, you can reduce the right margin slightly.*

4 ▪ Printing selected records as a report

Using a filter

▪ Click **Reports** in the objects bar, select the name of the report from which you wish to print certain records then click the ![Design] button to see the report's design.

▪ Show the report's property sheet by clicking the ![icon] tool button then click the square at the intersection of the horizontal and vertical rulers (![icon]).

▪ Click the **Data** tab on the report property sheet and in the **Filter** property, give the SQL statement that will extract the required records. The simplest type of SQL statement is **field name = value**.

*When the report is being created, if the source table or query already has a saved filter, the expression of that filter will appear automatically in the **Filter** property.*

▪ Activate the **Yes** option in the **Filter On** property.

 *If a sort order has already been saved with the report's source table or query when the report is created, this order appears automatically in the **Order By** property. You can use the **Order By On** property to activate or deactivate this sort order.*

Using a query

▪ Click **Reports** in the objects bar, select the name of the report from which you wish to print certain records then click the ![Design] button to see the report's design.

▪ Show the report's property sheet by clicking the ![icon] tool button then click the square at the intersection of the horizontal and vertical rulers (![icon]).

- Click the **Data** tab on the report property sheet and in the **Record Source** property, select the name of the query you wish to use to extract certain records.

  Of course, the query must make use of the existing fields in the report.

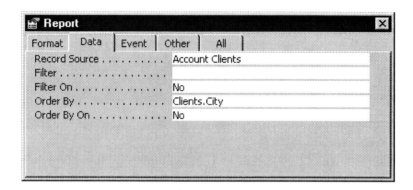

- Save the report by clicking the ▦ tool button.
- Open the print preview and/or start printing the report.
- Close the report using the **File - Close** command.

Below you can see **Practice Exercise** 4.2. This exercise is made up of 4 steps. If you do not know how to complete one of the steps, go back to the lesson to refer to the corresponding title. When you have finished, check your work by reading the **Solution** on the next page.

Steps that are likely to be tested in the exam are marked with a ▦ symbol. It is however recommended that you follow the whole exercise in order to gain a complete understanding of the lesson.

☞ Practice Exercise 4.2

To work through exercise 4.2, open the **4-2 BookBase.mdb** database located in the **MOUS Access 2000** folder.

▦ 1. Create a report from the **Clients** table, using a wizard:

- add all the fields from the Clients table to the report, except for the **Has Account** field,

- sort the records by **Last Name** in ascending order,

- the fields in the report should be laid out one next to the other, with a **Landscape** orientation and each record should print out on a single page,

- apply a **Casual** style to the report,

- the text **Client List** should appear in the report's title bar.

2. Define a sort order for the **Client List** report, sorting first by **City** then by **Last Name** then group the records by the **City** field, using an interval value of 1.

Save the changes made to the Client List report. Display this report in **Print Preview** view to see the result then close the report.

3. Preview the **Client List** report then print two copies of pages **4** to **6**. Make sure you print out two distinct copies, rather than page by page.

4. In the **Client List** report, use the **Account Clients** query to print a list of clients who have customer accounts. Save the changes made to the **Client List** report then display it in **Print Preview** view to see the result. Finish by closing the report.

If you want to put what you have learned into practice in a real document you can work on summary exercise 4 for the CREATING FORMS AND REPORTS section that can be found at the end of this book.

It is often possible to perform a task in several different ways, but here only the most efficient solution is presented. You can go back to the lesson if you wish to see the other techniques that can be used.

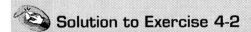

Solution to Exercise 4-2

1. To use the wizard to create a report based on the Clients table, start by clicking **Reports** in the objects bar then click the **New** button. Click the **Report Wizard** option. Open the drop-down list, select the **Clients** table then click **OK**. Add all the fields from the Clients table by clicking the **>>** button. Next, click the **<** button to remove the **Has Account** field from the **Selected Fields** list then click **Next** twice. Open the first list box, select the **Last Name** field then click **Next**. Leave the **Tabular** option active, activate the **Landscape** option then make sure the **Adjust the field width so all fields fit on a page** option is active. Click **Next**. Select the **Casual** style then click **Next**. Enter the text **Client List** in the text box and click the **Finish** button.

2. To sort the records in the Client List report by City then by Last Name in ascending order, click the **tool button** to see the report's design then click . Click the row selector on the **Last Name** field then press the **Insert** key. Click the first list box in the **Field/Expression** column then select the **City** field. For both the **City** and **Last Name** fields, leave the **Ascending** option active in the **Sort Order** column.

   To group the records by the City field, with an interval value of 1, make sure the **City** field is selected in the top half of the dialog box then choose **Yes** in the **Group Header** and **Group Footer** properties. Leave the **Each Value** option selected for the **Group On** property and the option **1** in the **Group Interval** property. Click the tool button to close the **Sorting and Grouping** dialog box.

To save the changes you have made to the Client List report, click the 🖫 tool button.

To display the report in Print Preview view, click the 🔍▾ tool button then close it with the **File - Close** command.

3. To preview the Client List report, click **Reports** in the objects bar then double-click the **Client List** report icon.

To print two copies of pages 4 to 6, activate the **File - Print** command. Type **4** in the **From** text box and **6** in the **To** text box in the **Print Range** frame. Then, enter **2** in the **Number of Copies** box (in the **Copies** frame) then tick the **Collate** option to print two complete copies of pages 4 to 6. Start printing by clicking **OK**.

To close the **Client List** report, activate the **File - Close** command.

4. To use the Account Clients query to print a list of clients with accounts, from the Client List report, click the 📈▾ tool button to display the report's design. Click the 🖼 tool button then click the square at the intersection of the horizontal and vertical rulers to see the Client List report's property sheet. Next, click the **Data** tab and in the **Record Source** property, select the **Account Clients** query.

To save the changes made to the Client List report then show it in **Print Preview** view, click first the 🖫 tool button then click 🔍▾.

To close the **Client List** report, use the **File - Close** command.

DESIGN VIEW
Lesson 5.1: Creating controls

1 ▪ Inserting a text box

*A **text box** is a bound control that displays the value of a field in a form or report.*

※ Show the design of the report or form in which you want to insert a text box (activate Design view: ⌖).

※ Click the ▣ tool button to display the field list.

※ Drag the name of the required field from the field list onto the place on the form or report where you wish to insert it.

Depending on the default properties associated with the text box tool, a label may be automatically inserted with the text box.

※ If you do not need it, delete the accompanying label then adjust the position, size and characteristics of the text box as required.

※ To close the window containing the field list, click the ☒ button or click the ▣ tool button again.

※ Save the changes made to the form or report then if necessary, close it with the **File - Close** command.

 You can insert several fields in a single action:
 - to select several adjacent fields within the field list, select the first field then hold down ⸂Shift⸃ while you select the last,
 - to select nonadjacent fields, select the first field then hold down the ⸂Ctrl⸃ key while you select the other field,
 - to select all the fields, double-click the field list's title bar.

2 ▪ Inserting a field as a check box, an option button or a toggle button

Check boxes, option buttons and toggle buttons are used to manage Yes/No fields. The check box is the default presentation for a Yes/No field.

▪ Display in Design view (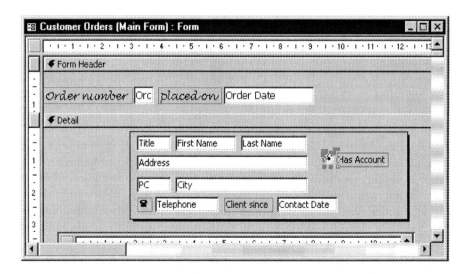) the form or report in which you wish to insert the check box, option button or toggle button.

▪ If necessary, show the toolbox by clicking the tool button.

▪ Select the tool that corresponds to the presentation you want for the control: (check box), (option button), (toggle button).

▪ If necessary, click the tool button to display the field list.

▪ In the list, click the **Yes/No** type field concerned and drag it to where you want to insert it in the form or report.

- If you insert a toggle button, click inside it, enter the text it should display then confirm by pressing the ⏎ key.

  *The text you enter subsequently appears in the **Caption** property on the **Format** page of the toggle button's property sheet. This button has a raised appearance.*

- If you wish, modify the presentation of the check box, option button or toggle button.

- Click the 🖫 tool button to save the changes.

  📄 *You can also place several check boxes, option buttons or toggle buttons in an option group; you would then select one of the values displayed in that group.*

  If a Yes/No field contains a Yes value (or True or On), its check box is ticked, its option button contains a dot and its toggle button appears pressed-in. If the filed value is No (or False or Off), its check box or option button is empty and the toggle button appears raised.

3 ▪ Creating a list of values

*Access provides two tools which make it possible to select data from a list instead of typing it in: the **list box** and the **combo box**. These two types of control present a list of values from which you select the value of your field: with a combo box, it is also possible to enter a value that is not in the list. To create this type of control you must define certain properties. It is a good idea to let the Control Wizard guide you if you are unfamiliar with the process.*

- Open the form concerned and display it in Design view.

- Click the 🛠 tool button to display the toolbox, if it is hidden.

- If necessary, click the 🔧 tool button to activate the Control Wizard.

- Click the ⊞ tool button to create a list box or the ⊞ tool button to create a combo box.

- Drag to draw the outline of the control.

  Access activates the List Box or Combo Box Wizard.

- Activate the **I will type in the values that I want** option then click the **Next** button.

- Enter the number of columns for the value list then click the first empty cell in **Col1**.

- Enter the values in the list as you would in a datasheet: the ⇥ key can be used to go to the next cell.

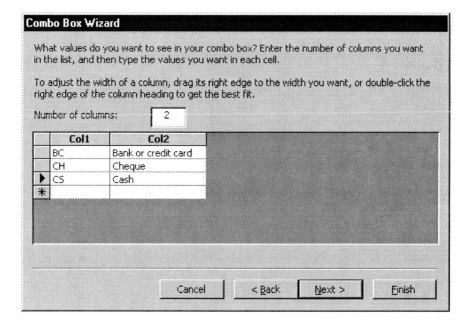

- Click **Next** to go to the next step.

- Activate the **Store that value in this field** option then select the field for which you are creating the list.

※ Click **Next**.

※ Give the text for the field label then click the **Finish** button.

※ To see the properties for the list of values, click the ▣ tool button then click the **Data** tab. The **Row Source Type** property shows **Value List**, the values in the list appear in the **Row Source** property, separated by semi-colons and the number of columns in the list can be seen in the **Column Count** property on the **Format** page.

If you create a list of values without the help of the Control Wizard, you will have to define these properties yourself.

※ Click the 💾 tool button to save your changes.

📄 *With a combo box, you can also enter data of your choice, providing that the **Limit To List** property on the **Data** page is deactivated.*

🖱 *A list box or combo box can also be defined in the Design view of a table, using the **Lookup** page in the field properties.*

🄴4 ▪ Creating a list of data from other tables

In a form which contains data from several tables, you can insert a list box comprising values from one or more fields in one of these tables.

※ Show the form in Design view.

※ Click the 🔨 tool button to display the toolbox, if it is hidden.

※ If necessary, click the 🖾 tool button to activate the Control Wizard.

- Click the ⊞ tool button to create a list box or the ⊞ tool button to create a combo box.

- Drag to draw the outline of the control.

   The List Box or Combo Box Wizard will help you to define the control's characteristics.

- If necessary, activate the first option then click the **Next** button to go to the next step.

- In the **View** frame, click the type of object wish you want to see.

- Select the table or query containing the values you want to insert in the list then click the **Next** button.

- Select the field(s) whose values should appear in the list box.

   One of these fields must be common to both the selected table and the source of the active form.

- Click the **Next** button.

- Deactivate the **Hide key column (recommended)** option if you want the column containing the primary key values to be visible.

- If necessary, modify the list's column widths by dragging the right edges of the columns concerned then click **Next**.

- Select the field in the form's source whose value you want to store.

   *This step is only available if the **Hide key column** option is deactivated.*

- Click the **Next** button.

- Activate the **Store that value in this field** option then select the field in the form's source where you want to store the value.

- Click the **Next** button.

- Enter the text of the label associated with the list box then click the **Finish** button.

» To see the list box's properties, click the 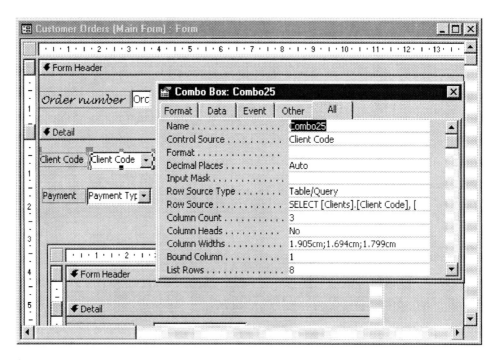 tool button then click the **All** page on the property sheet to see the properties set up by the wizard when the list box was created.

» These are the properties you would have to define yourself, if you chose not to use the wizard:

Control Source the name of the field associated with the control.

Row Source Type choose **Table/Query**.

Row Source name of the table or query which contains the field values or the SQL instruction allowing the fields inserted in the list to be selected. If only a table name or query name is specified, the columns in the list will contain the values of the first x fields of the table or query, with x corresponding to the number of columns.

Column Count	the number of columns in the list.
Column Heads	activate this option to display the column headings (field names) in the list.
Column Widths	the widths of the columns in the list, separated by a semicolon. If a column's width is 0, it is not visible.
Bound Column	the number of the column containing the values which are common to the source of the list and the source of the form.
List Rows	the number of rows visible.
List Width	the sum of the column widths.
Limit To List	For a combo box, enter **No** so you can also enter any other value.

▪ Click the 🖫 tool button to save the changes made.

⌨5 ▪ **Creating a calculated control**

You can use this technique in a form or report to show a value that is calculated from one or more fields.

▪ Show in Design view (⟨✏️⟩) the form or report in which you want to create a calculated control.

▪ If necessary, click the ⚒ tool button to display the toolbox then click the abl tool button.

▪ Drag to draw the control's frame.

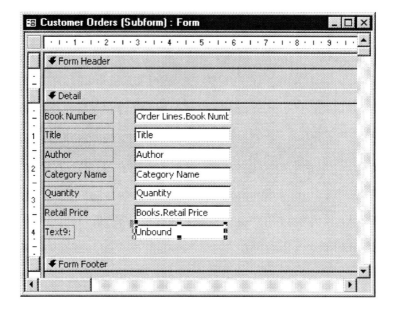

A control created in this way is unbound, as it is not linked to any field in the source table.

- Click the 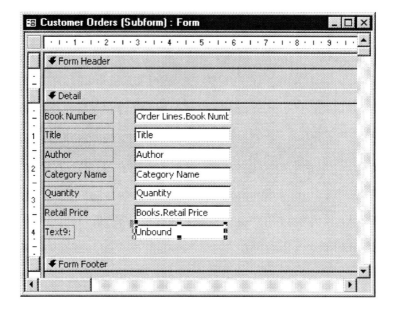 tool button to show the control's property sheet.

- Click the **Other** tab and give the **Name** for the control in the corresponding property.

  You cannot use the name of an existing control!

- Click the **Data** tab then type an equals sign (=) in the **Control Source** property.

- Enter the expression that Access will use to calculate the control value or click the button to start the Expression Builder. This expression can include:

  - the name(s) of one or more fields in the source table (field names must be placed in square brackets),

  - mathematical operators: * (to multiply), + (to add), - (to subtract), / (to divide any number), \ (to divide one integer by another (the result is the part of the value that is a whole number)), ^ (to raise to a power ($2 \char94 3 = 8$)), Mod (to calculate the remainder when a number is divided).

- parentheses to indicate the order in which operations should be performed,

- the concatenation operator &,

- text (which should be entered between quotation marks),

- various functions (mathematical, statistical etc):

Iif()	calculates the expression according to one or more conditions,
Date()	calculates the control date.
Sum()	calculates the sum of the values in a field,
Average()	calculates the average of the values in a field,
...	

For example:

[Price]*[Tax]	calculates the amount of tax
[Price]*(1+[Tax])	calculates the price including tax
[Title]&" "&![Surname]	concatenates the Title and Surname fields
Month([Contact Date])	extracts the month from the value in the Contact Date field
Sum([Quantity])	calculates the sum of the values in the Quantity field.
Average([Price]*(1+[Tax]))	calculates the average tax-inclusive price

» Click the ⊞ tool button to save the changes made.

🗋 *In a report with grouped records, the location of your expression determines on which records it performs its calculation.*

⊞6 ▪ **Inserting an option group into a form**

The three salespeople shown on the form below make up an option group:

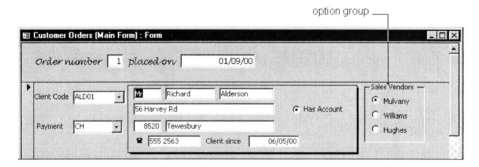

- Display the form in Design view.

- If necessary, click the [⟋] tool button to activate the Control Wizard.

- If it is hidden, display the toolbox with the [⚒] tool button then click the [xyz] tool button.

- Drag to draw the outline of the option group control.

  Access starts the Option Group Wizard.

- Enter the text for each label in the option group as in a datasheet, pressing [⇥] or [↓] to go to the next cell.

- Click **Next**.

- If you wish, choose the value that will be active by default from the list of labels then click **Next**.

- Indicate the value you wish to assign to each option in the group.

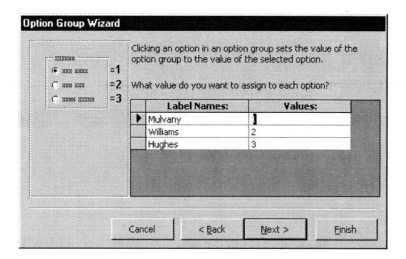

These are the values that will be stored in the table. This must be numerical data: an option group can only be created for number type fields (or AutoNumber).

» Click **Next**.

» Activate the **Store that value in this field** option then select the corresponding field.

» Click **Next**.

» Select the type of button you want to use then the style of frame.

As a rule, option buttons are used when only one option in the group can be activated at a time.

» Click **Next**.

» Enter the text for the group label in the appropriate box then click the **Finish** button.

The options within the group are presented one beneath the other.

» To see the properties of a button in the group, click that button to select it then click the [icon] tool button to show its property sheet. Click the **Data** tab: the **Option Value** property determines the value stored in the form's source table when a user chooses that button.

⊗ Click the ⊡ tool button to save the changes made.

🗐 7 ▪ **Creating a text label**

⊗ Display in Design view (⬚▾) the form or report in which you wish to insert a label.

⊗ If it is hidden, display the toolbox with the ⬚ tool button.

⊗ Click to select the Aa tool button.

When the mouse pointer is positioned in the form, it takes the shape of a letter A.

⊗ Drag to draw the outline of the label.

As you drag you can see the size of the label on the ruler. The insertion point flashes inside the frame.

⊗ Type the text for the label: use Shift⏎ if you wish to make a line break.

⊗ Confirm with ⏎.

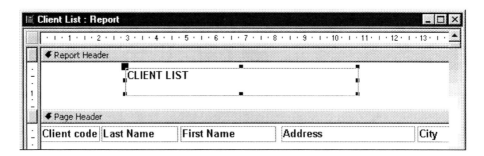

You have created an unbound control. By default, the text in the label is aligned on the left.

⊗ Click the ⊡ tool button to save the changes made.

Each time you use a tool, the ⬚ *tool becomes once again the active tool. If you want a tool to remain active so you can use it more than once, select it with a double-click.*

To modify the text in a label, click to select the label concerned, then point to the text in the label and when the pointer takes the form of a capital "i" (I) click. Make the required changes then enter.

⊞8 ▪ Drawing a rectangle or a line

▪ Show in Design view (⬚) the form or report in which you wish to draw a rectangle or line.

▪ If it is hidden, display the toolbox with the ⬚ tool button.

▪ Click the ⬚ tool button if you want to draw a rectangle or the ⬚ tool button to draw a line.

▪ Drag to draw the required shape.

The drawn object appears in the foreground.

▪ Click the ⬚ tool button to save the changes made.

9 ▪ Managing a tab control

Creating a tab control

This control is made up of two pages:

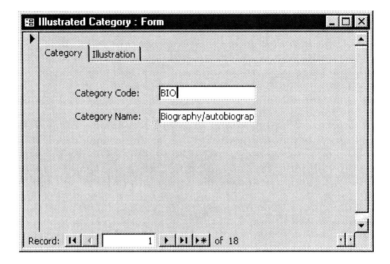

* Click **Forms** in the objects bar, select the name of the form in which you want to create a tab control then click the [Design] button to see its design.

* If it is hidden, display the toolbox with the tool button.

* Click the tool button then drag to draw the tab control in the form window.

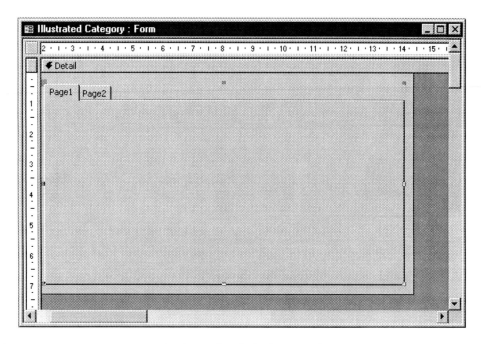

Access inserts two pages, which are by default named Page"n".

* To go to a page, click its tab.

* If necessary, click the 🔲 tool button to show the field list then insert the required controls on each of the pages.

* If you wish, modify the presentation of these controls.

* Click the 💾 tool button to save the changes made.

📄 *You can insert any type of control into a tab control page, except for another tab control!*
Each page plus the tab control itself have specific properties. To show a page's property sheet, click the tab then click the 🖼 tool button; to show the tab control's properties, click the blank space to the right of the tabs.

Managing tab control pages

* To rename a page, click its tab then click the 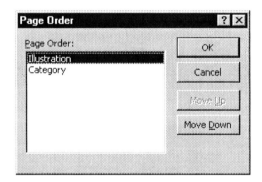 tool button to see its property sheet. Next, click the **Format** tab and enter the new name in the **Caption** property.

* To insert a new page, right-click a tab and choose the **Insert Page** option.

* To delete a page, right-click its tab and choose the **Delete Page** option.

* To modify the page order, right-click any tab and choose the **Page Order** option.

Page Order	? X
Page Order:	OK
Illustration	Cancel
Category	
	Move Up
	Move Down

* Click the name of the page you wish to move and click either the **Move Up** or **Move Down** button.

* Click **OK**.

10 • Inserting a page break

Inserting a page break in a form or report ensures that a new page starts at that point on the printed copy.

* Show in Design view (▭ ▾) the form or report in which you want to add a page break.

* If it is hidden, display the toolbox with the 🛠 tool button.

* Click the [≡] tool button.

* In the window, click the place where Access should make a page break.

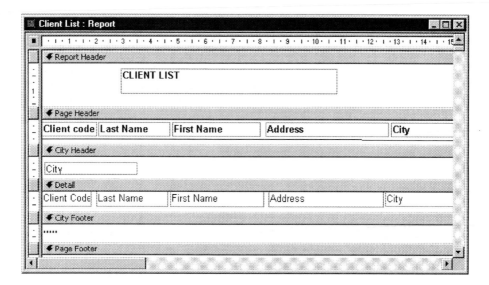

A page break is represented by a thick dotted line (as seen here in the **City Footer** section).

No matter where you click, the page break control always appears at the far left of the line.

* Click the [💾] tool button to save the changes made.

11 ▪ **Inserting a picture**

The picture will be visible on all the pages of the form or report; it is not linked to a field in the table or to an external object.

* Show in Design view ([⬚ ▾]) the form or report in which you want to insert a picture.

⁎ If it is hidden, display the toolbox with the ⊞ tool button.

⁎ Click the ⊞ tool button.

⁎ Drag to draw the outline for the picture.

⁎ Select the drive then the folder in which the image file is stored then double-click the document's name.

The image can be in vector format (wmf, cgm…) or bitmap format (bmp, pcx, tif…).

⁎ Click the ⊞ tool button to save the changes made.

▥12 ▪ Inserting an object

Inserting a bound object

*The object is linked to an **OLE Object** type field (OLE stands for Object Linking and Embedding). **OLE Object** type fields are used to insert into a form an object made in another Windows application (this can be an image made in a drawing application such as Paint, a table created in Excel etc).*

*This application must be a **server** application, with Access being the **client** application. The OLE technique is specific to the Windows environment and works on the principle of an object created in a server application being inserted in a client application. This result is brought about by one of two methods:*

*- by **embedding** the object. The inserted object becomes an integral part of the destination document; it can only be modified by first opening that document.*

*- by **linking** the object. In this case, the object does not actually exist in the destination document; instead the document contains a linking formula that allows it to display the linked object when necessary. The object can be modified in the server application, independently of the client application (you can then choose how you wish to update the destination document).*

⁎ Show the form in Design view.

* If it is hidden, display the toolbox with the ⬚ tool button then click the ⬚ tool button.

* Drag to draw the outline for the bound object.

* Click the ⬚ tool button to show the bound object's property sheet then click the **Data** tab.

* In the **Control Source** property, choose a source for the bound object; this must be an **OLE Object** type field.

* If necessary, modify the text for the control's label. To do this, click to select the label, click in the text then make the required changes and press the ⮐ key.

* Click the ⬚ tool button to show the form in Form view.

* Using the arrows in the bottom left corner of the form, display the record in which you wish to insert the object.

* Click to select the object frame within the record.

* **Insert - Object**

   The dialog box contains a list of the type of objects you could insert (this list depends on the applications installed on your computer).

* If you need to create the object in the application, check that the **Create New** option is active, select the **Object type** you wish to insert then click **OK**. Create the object then click in the form.
   To select an existing object, click the **Create from File** option. Next, click the **Browse** button and double-click to select the required file.

* Activate the **Link** option if you want to establish a link between the Access document and the object, rather than simply embedding it.

* Activate the **Display as Icon** option if you want just the file icon to appear in the Access document.

* Click **OK**.

* Click the ⬚ tool button to save the changes made then close the form using **File - Close**.

To delete the object, click in the object frame and press Del *.*

Modifying a bound object

* Display the form in Form view and go to the record concerned.
* Double-click the object to start the server application.

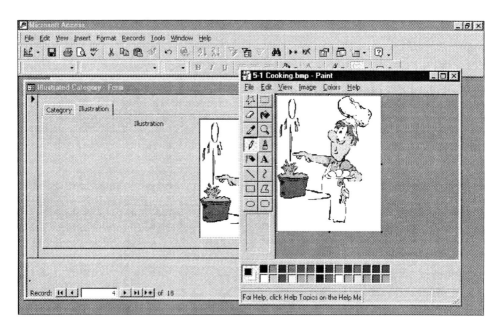

If a link exists between the object and the document containing it, the object appears in a separate window. If the object is embedded, you can modify it using "in-place editing": the menus and tools of the server application temporarily replace those of Access so you can modify the object.

* Make the required changes.
* For an embedded object, click anywhere in the client application window to retrieve the menus and tools of the client application.

For a linked object, close the server application window, saving the changes made.

Managing OLE links

If the link is automatic, the object is updated automatically when you open the form or report. If the link is manual, you must tell Access when to update the object.

» Click **Forms** in the objects bar then double-click the icon of the form containing the OLE links you wish to work with.

» To update an object, select it then use the **Edit - OLE/DDE Links** command.

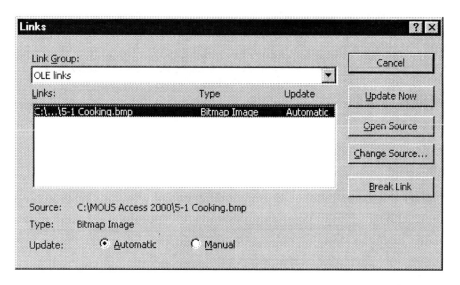

» Select the name of the document concerned then click the **Update Now** button.

» To modify the type of link, activate either **Automatic** or **Manual**.

» Click the ⊠ button to close the **Links** dialog box.

» Click the 🖫 tool button to save the changes made then close the form with the **File - Close** command.

You can also change the type of link by displaying the property sheet of the control concerned and in the **Update Options** property on the **Data** page, choose either **Automatic** or **Manual**

Inserting an unbound object

This type of object will appear on each page of the form or report and is not linked to any field in a table.

* Show in Design view (▨ ▾) the form or report in which you wish to insert an unbound object.

* If it is hidden, display the toolbox by clicking the ⚒ tool button.

* Click the ▦ tool button then drag to draw the object's outline in the form window.

   The **Insert Object** dialog box appears on the screen, as when you insert a bound object.

* Continue inserting the object following the same procedure as for a bound object.

 To modify an unbound object, show the form's design then double-click the object: the menus and tools from the server application temporarily replace those in Access. Make the required changes then click elsewhere in the form window to retrieve the Access menus and toolbars.

Below you can see **Practice Exercise** 5.1. This exercise is made up of 12 steps. If you do not know how to complete one of the steps, go back to the lesson to refer to the corresponding title. When you have finished, check your work by reading the **Solution** on the next page.

All the steps in this exercise are likely to be tested in the exam.

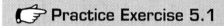

Practice Exercise 5.1

*To work through exercise 5.1, open the **5-1 BookBase.mdb** database located in the **MOUS Access 2000** folder.*

1. Insert the **Category Code, Retail Price** and **Number of Pages** text boxes in the **Enter Books** form as shown below. Save and close the form.

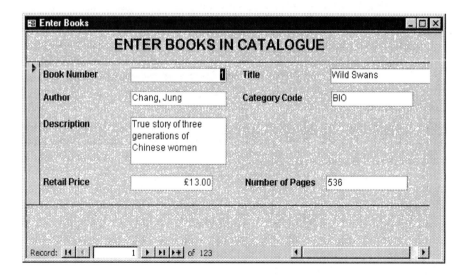

2. In the **Customer Orders (Main Form)** form, insert the **Has Account** field as an option button as shown below then save and close the form:

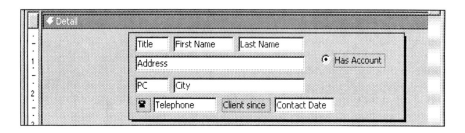

3. Using the wizard, insert a combo box (using a fixed list of values) in the **Customer Orders (Main Form)** form. You should take into account the following details:

- you should insert the combo box to the left of the **Postcode** text box, as shown below:

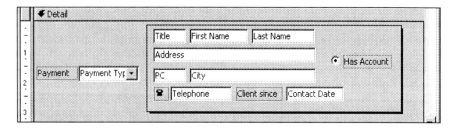

- **2** columns are required for the list, and the contents should be as follows:

BC	Bank or credit card
CH	Cheque
CS	Cash

- the first column contains the value that should be stored in the databases.

- the list values should be stored in the **Payment Type** field.

- the text for the field label is **Payment**.

Save the changes made to the form then display the form in Form view. Open the **Payment** drop-down list to view its contents then return to Design view.

4. In the **Customer Orders (Main Form)** form, create a combo box with the wizard. Take into account the following details:

- the combo box should be inserted to the left of the **Title** text box as seen here:

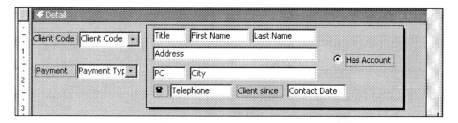

- the **Client Code**, **First Name** and **Last Name** fields in the **Clients** table contain the values to include in the combo box.

- the column containing the primary key values should be visible.

- the **Client Code** column contains the values to be stored in the database.

- the **Client Code** field is the field in the form's source in which the value should be stored.

- the text for the list box label is **Client Code**.

Save the changes made to the form then display it in Form view. Open the **Client Code** combo box to view its contents then close the form.

5. Under the **Retail Price** text box in the **Customer Orders (Subform)** form, create a calculated control called **Total** that will calculate the total amount per line (per book number). Save the changes made to the form then display it in Form view. Go to record **10** to check if the expression is correct then close the form.

6. Using the wizard, insert an option group in the **Customer Orders (Main Form)** form, taking into account the following details:

   - the option group should be inserted to the right of the frame containing the client identification fields (title, last name etc) as seen below:

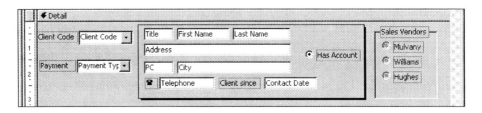

   - the labels for the option group are **Mulvany**, **Williams** and **Hughes** in that order.

   - set the active default option as **Williams**.

   - the value **1** is assigned to the **Mulvany** option, the value **2** is assigned to the **Williams** option and the value **3** is assigned to the **Hughes** option.

   - the value selected in the option group should be stored in the **Vendor Number** field.

   - use an **Option** type of button with a **Sunken** style.

   - the text for the option group label is **Sales Vendors**.

   Save the changes made to the form then display it in Form view. Scroll through the first 6 records to view the option group then close the form.

7. Create a label containing the text **CLIENT LIST** in the header of the **Client List** report.

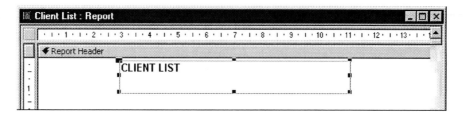

Save the changes made to the report, display it in Print Preview view then return to the report's design.

8. Draw a straight line across the width of the report window beneath the labels in the **Page Header** section in the **Client List** report.

Save the changes made to the report, view it in Print Preview view then close it.

9. Create a tab control with two pages, **14 cm** wide and **6.5 cm** high (or 5 ½ by 2 ½ inches), in the Detail section of the **Illustrated Category** form. Insert the **Category Code** and **Category Name** text boxes into the second page of the tab control as shown below:

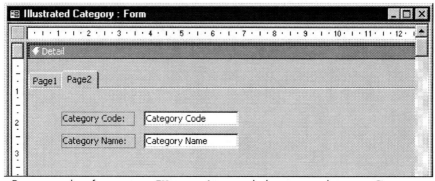

Rename the first page **Illustration** and the second page **Category** then move the **Category** page in front of the **Illustration** page.

Save the changes made to the form, display it in Form view then close it.

10. Insert a page break in the **Client List** report so each new group starts on a new page. Display the report in Print Preview view, adjust the zoom level then scroll through the first three pages. Save the changes made to the report then close it.

11. In the **Enter Books** form, insert the picture called **5-1 Reading.bmp** located in the **MOUS Access 2000** folder, as shown below:

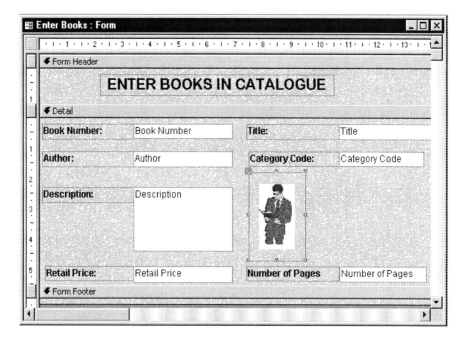

Save the changes made to the form, display it in Form view then scroll through the first five records and close the form.

12.In the **Illustrated Category** form, insert as bound objects **5-1 Cooking.bmp**, **5-1 Crime.bmp** and **5-1 Travel.bmp** from the **MOUS Access 2000** folder, following these instructions:

- insert the bound object control into the **Illustration** page as shown below:

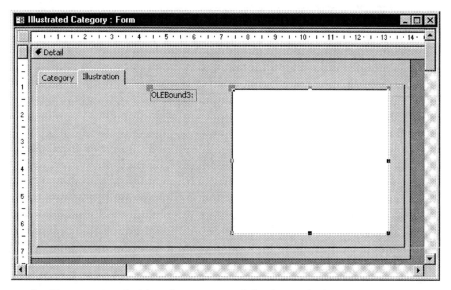

- the **Illustration** field is the source of the bound object.

- the caption for the label associated with the bound object control is **Illustration**.

- insert the **5-1 Cooking.bmp** object into the 4th record, the **5-1 Crime.bmp** object into the 5th record and the **5-1 Travel.bmp** object into the 17th record.

- for each object, you should create a link between the Access document and the object.

Save the changes made to the form then close it.

If you want to put what you have learned into practice in a real document you can work on summary exercise 5 for the DESIGN VIEW section that can be found at the end of this book.

It is often possible to perform a task in several different ways, but here only the most efficient solution is presented. You can go back to the lesson if you wish to see the other techniques that can be used.

Solution to Exercise 5.1

1. To insert the Category Code, Retail Price and Number of Pages text boxes into the Enter Books form, click **Forms** in the objects bar and select the **Enter Books** form. Click the 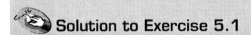 button then the ⊟ tool button to display the field list.

   To insert the Category Code text box, click the **Category Code** field in the field list then drag it beneath the **Title** text box.

   To insert the Retail Price text box, click the **Retail Price** field in the field list then drag it beneath the **Description** text box.

   To insert the Number of Pages text box, click the **Number of Pages** field in the field list then drag it beneath the **Retail Price** text box.

   To save then close the Enter Books form, click the 🖫 tool button then use the **File - Close** command.

2. To insert the Has Account field into the Customer Orders (Main Form) form in the shape of an option button, click **Forms** in the objects bar, select the **Customer Orders (Main Form)** form then click the ⌕ Design button. Click the ⚒ tool button to display the toolbox then the ⊟ tool button to display the field list.

   Activate the ⦿ tool button then drag the **Has Account** field from the field list onto the form, to the right of the **Address** text box.

   To save the changes made to the form, click the 🖫 tool button.

3. To create with a wizard a combo box of fixed values in the Customer Orders (Main Form) form, activate the [tool] tool if it is not active then click the [tool] tool button. Draw the outline of the control as shown in step 3. Activate the **I will type in the values that I want** option and click **Next**. Type **2** in the **Number of columns** box then click the first cell in the **Col1** column. Type **BC**, press the [key] key, type **Bank or credit card**; press the [key] key. Type **CH**, press the [key] key, type **Cheque**; press the [key] key. Type **CS**, press the [key] key and type **Cash**; click the **Next** button. Select the **Col1** field in the list box then click **Next**. Activate the **Store that value in this field** option, select the **Payment Type** field in the drop-down list box then click **Next**. Enter **Payment** in the text box and click the **Finish** button.

To save the changes made to the form, click [tool]. To show the form in Form view, click the [tool] tool button.

To open the **Payment** list box to view its contents, click the black triangle that appears on the right side of the list box.

To return to the form in Design view, click the [tool] tool button.

4. To create a combo box to the left of the Title text box in the Customer Orders (Main Form) form, click the [tool] tool button in the toolbox then drag to draw the outline of the control (use the illustration in step 4 to help you). Leave the first option active then click **Next**. Select the **Clients** table then click **Next**. Double-click the **Client Code**, **First Name** and **Last Name** fields then click **Next**. Deactivate the **Hide key column (recommended)** option and click **Next**. Select the **Client Code** column in the list box and click **Next**. Activate the **Store that value in this field** option, select the **Client Code** field in the drop-down list box then click **Next**. Enter **Client Code** in the text box and click the **Finish** button.

To save the changes made to the form and display it in Form view, click first the [tool] tool button then click [tool].

To open the Client Code list to see its contents, click the black triangle on the **Client Code** list box.

Close the form by activating the **File - Close** command.

5. To create under the Retail Price text box in the Customer Orders (Subform) form a calculated control that will add up the total amount due per order line (for each book number), click **Forms** in the objects bar. Select the **Customer Orders (Subform)** form and click the [⚞ Design] button. Click the [abl] tool button then drag to draw the control's outline underneath the **Retail Price** text box. If necessary, click the [☞] tool button to show the control's properties then click the **Other** tab. Enter **Total** in the **Name** property then click the **Data** tab. Click the **Control Source** property and enter the expression **=[Quantity]*[Retail Price]**.

To save the changes made to the form and display it in Form view, click first the [💾] tool button then open the list on the [▦ ▾] tool button and click the **Form View** option.

To go to record 10, select the record number in the bottom left corner of the window then enter **10** and press [↵].
To close the form, use the **File - Close** command.

6. To insert an option group in the Customer Orders (Main Form) form, using a wizard, click **Forms** in the objects bar and select the **Customer Orders (Main Form)** form. Click the [⚞ Design] button. Click the [▢] tool button in the toolbox the drag to draw a frame for the option group control, using the picture in step 6 to guide you. Enter **Mulvany**, and press the [⇥] key; enter **Williams** and press the [⇥] key again then type **Hughes** and click the **Next** button. Open the drop-down list on the **Yes, the default choice is** option and choose **Williams**. Click **Next** twice. Activate the **Store the value in this field** option then select the **Vendor Number** field in the drop-down list and click **Next**. Activate the **Option buttons** and **Sunken** options then click **Next**. Enter **Sales Vendors** in the text box and click the **Finish** button.

To save the changes made to the form and display it in Form view, click first the [icon] tool button then the [icon] tool button.

To scroll through the first six records to see how the option group works, click the [icon] button in the bottom left corner of the window six times.

Close the form by activating the **File - Close** command.

7. To create a label containing the text CLIENT LIST in the report header of the Client List report, start by clicking **Reports** in the objects bar and select the **Client List** report. Click the [Design] button. Click the [Aa] tool button in the toolbox then drag to draw the control as shown in step 7. Enter the text **CLIENT LIST** and press the [icon] key.

To save the changes made to the report, click the [icon] tool button. To show it in Print Preview view, click the [icon] tool button.

To return to the report's design, click the [icon] tool button.

8. To draw a line across the width of the report window beneath the labels in the Page Header section of the Client List report, click the [icon] tool button. Drag from the left side of the window, beneath the **Client code** label in the **Page Header** section, towards the right until you reach the right hand side of the window.

To save the changes made to the report then display it in Print Preview view, click first the [icon] tool button then [icon].

To close the report, use the **File - Close** command.

9. To create a tab control with two pages, 14 cm wide by 6.5 cm high in the Illustrated Category form, click **Forms** in the objects bar then select the **Illustrated Category** form. Click the Design button. Click the tool button, then drag from the top left corner of the **Detail** section towards the right to the **14 cm** mark and downwards to the **6.5 cm** mark.

To insert the Category Code and Category Name text boxes into the second page of the control, click the **Page2** tab then click the tool button to show the field list.

To insert the Category Code text box, drag the **Category Code** field from the field list onto the **Detail** section of the form window, as shown in step 9. To insert the Category Name text box, drag the **Category Name** field from the field list onto the **Detail** section of the form window, as the illustration shows in step 9.

To rename the first tab control page Illustration, click the **Page1** tab then click the tool button to show the page's property sheet. Click the **Format** tab and enter **Illustration** in the **Caption** property.

To rename the second tab control page Category, click the **Page2** tab, then enter **Category** in the **Caption** property.

To move the Category page in front of the Illustration page, right-click the **Illustration** tab then choose the **Page Order** option. Click the **Move Down** button then click **OK**.

To save the changes made to the form then display it in Form view, click first the tool button then .

To close the form, use the **File - Close** command.

10. To insert a page break into the Client List report, so each new group starts on a new page, click **Reports** in the objects bar, select the **Client List** report and click the Design button. Click the tool button in the toolbox then click the **City Footer** section.

To show the report in Print Preview view, adjust the zoom and look at the first three pages, start by clicking the [icon] tool button. Click the preview window then click the [▶] button in the bottom left corner of the window three times.

To save the changes made to the report and close it, use the **File - Save** command then **File - Close**.

11. To insert into the Enter Books form the 5-1 Reading.bmp file, located in the MOUS Access 2000 folder, click **Forms** in the objects bar then select the **Enter Books** form. Click the [Design] button. Click the [icon] tool button in the toolbox then drag to draw the outline for the picture as shown in step 11.

Select the **MOUS Access 2000** folder then click the **5-1 Reading.bmp** file and click **OK**.

To save the changes made to the form then display it in Form view, click the [icon] tool button then [icon].

To scroll through the first 5 records, click the [▶] button in the bottom left corner of the form window 5 times.

To close the form, use the **File - Close** command.

12. To insert in the Illustrated Category form as bound objects the 5-1 Cooking.bmp, 5-1 Travel.bmp and 5-1 Crime.bmp files from the MOUS Access 2000 folder, start by clicking **Forms** in the objects bar then select the **Illustrated Category** form and click the [Design] button. Click the **Illustration** tab then the [icon] tool button in the toolbox. Drag to draw the bound object frame as seen in step 12.

To define the bound object's source, click the [icon] tool button to show its property sheet then click the **Data** tab. Open the drop-down list on the **Control Source** property and select the **Illustration** field.

To use "Illustration" as the caption for the bound object's label, click the label to select it then select the text it contains and press ⬛Del. Enter the text **Illustration** and press the ⬛ key.

To insert the 5-1 Cooking.bmp object into the fourth record, click the ⬛▾ tool button to display the form in Form view. If necessary, click the **Illustration** tab to activate it then click the ⬛▶ button in the bottom left corner of the form three times until you are in the fourth record. Activate the **Insert - Object** command and choose the **Create from File** option. Click the **Browse** button and if necessary, select the **MOUS Access 2000** folder then double-click the **5-1 Cooking.bmp** file. Tick the **Link** option and click **OK**.

To insert the 5-1 Crime.bmp object into the fifth record, click the ⬛▶ button at the bottom of the form to go to that record. Activate the **Insert - Object** command and choose the **Create from File** option. Click the **Browse** button and if necessary, select the **MOUS Access 2000** folder then double-click the **5-1 Crime.bmp** file. Tick the **Link** option and click **OK**.

To insert the 5-1 Travel.bmp object into the 17th record, click the ⬛▶ button at the bottom of the form until you reach the 17th record. Activate the **Insert - Object** command and choose the **Create from File** option. Click the **Browse** button and if necessary, select the **MOUS Access 2000** folder then double-click the **5-1 Travel.bmp** file. Tick the **Link** option and click **OK**.

To save the form, click the ⬛ tool button then close it using the **File - Close** command.

DESIGN VIEW
Lesson 5.2: Controls and sections

1 ▪ Selecting controls

» Show the form or report in Design view (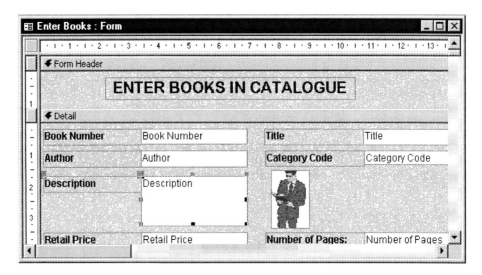) then make sure the 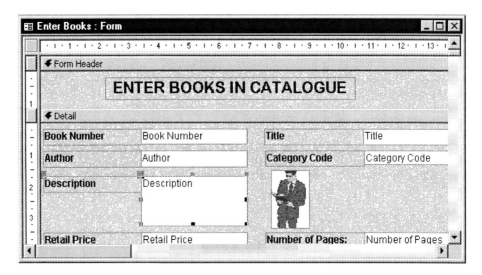 tool is active in the toolbox.

» To select a text box and its accompanying label, click the text box.

Handles appear around the selected elements.
*The name of the selected control appears in the **Formatting** toolbar. You can also use this list box to select an object by choosing it in the list.*

» To select a label without its text box, click just the label.

*In this case, **sizing handles** surround the label (the square in the top left corner of the control is called the move handle).*

» To select several adjacent controls, drag to draw an imaginary rectangle around them.

» To select non-adjacent controls, click the first control, hold down the Shift key then click the other controls to select them.

※ To select all the controls situated along a vertical or horizontal axis, click the ruler at that axis then drag along the ruler to extend the selection area.

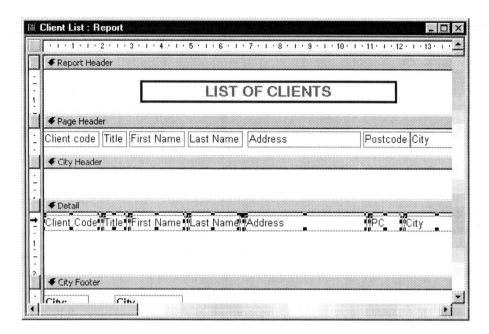

※ To cancel the current selection, click anywhere else in the form.

The **Selection behaviour** options, which can be found in **Tools - Options - Forms/Reports** tab, indicate whether you can partially enclose objects when making a multiple selection (this is the default option) or if you have to completely enclose them.

The **Select All** option in the **Edit** menu or Ctrl A can be used to select all the controls on the form or report. There is also an option you can use to **Select Form** or **Select Report**.

2 ▪ Copying/moving controls

Moving controls within a section

※ Display the form or report in Design view ( ) and make sure the tool is active in the toolbox.

※ Select the controls concerned.

※ To move a text box <u>and</u> its label, point to one of text box edges: the pointer takes the shape of a hand.

To move either the text box <u>or</u> the label, point to the control's **move handle**:

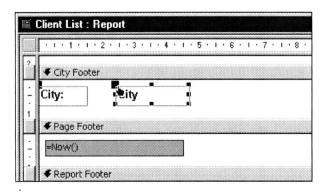

The pointer takes the shape of a hand with a pointing finger.

※ Drag the control to its new position; hold down the key if you don't want the control to be snapped (attracted) to the points on the magnetic grid.

※ Save the changes made to the form or report then close it.

📝 *If the **Snap to Grid** option is active in the **Format** menu, the controls will be attracted towards points on the window's magnetic grid when you move them (this makes them easier to line up).*

You can force controls to move in a horizontal or vertical line by holding down the [Shift] key as you drag them.

Copying/moving controls from one section to another

▪ Show the form or report concerned in Design view ( ) and make sure the tool button is active in the toolbox.

▪ Select the control(s) concerned.

▪ To copy data, use the **Edit - Copy** command or or [Ctrl] C.

To move data, use the **Edit - Move** command or or [Ctrl] X.

▪ Click the title bar of the section into which you wish to copy or move the data.

▪ **Edit - Paste** or or [Ctrl] V

▪ Save the changes made to the form or report then close it.

3 ▪ Deleting controls

▪ Show the form or report concerned in Design view ( ) then make sure the tool is active in the toolbox.

▪ Select the controls concerned. To delete a text box and its accompanying label, click the text box. To delete just a label without its text box, click the label.

▪ **Edit - Delete** or [Del]

▪ Save the changes made to the form or report then close it.

If you delete a text box, its associated label is deleted automatically.

🗐4 ▪ Resizing a control

* Show the form or report concerned in Design view (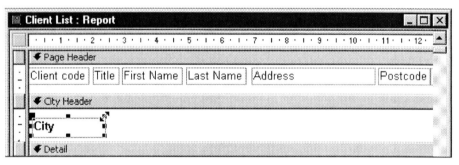) and make sure the 　tool button is active in the toolbox.

* Select the control concerned.

* Point to one of the sizing handles to modify either the width or the height. To modify the height and the width simultaneously, point to one of the corner handles.

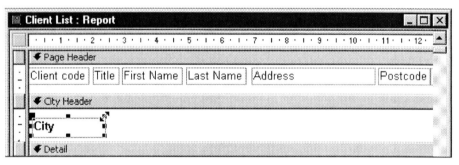

The pointer takes the form of a double-headed arrow.

* Drag to resize the control the release the mouse button.

When you resize a text box, its length, expressed as a number of characters, appears on the status bar: this value is linked to the font applied to the text box. The length of a text box can be greater than the field size. You should however make sure it is not smaller than the field size or a part of the field value may be cut off in the form.

* Save the changes made to the form or report then close it.

You can also adapt the size of a label to the length of text it contains; use the **Format - Size - To Fit** command.

If you activate the **Format - Size - To Grid** command, the corners of the selected control snap to the grid when you resize or move it.

To give a control a precise size, show that control's property sheet, click the **Format** tab then change the values in the **Width** and **Height** properties.

5 ▪ Formatting the text in a control

Changing the text alignment

▪ Show the form or report concerned in Design view ( ) and make sure the tool button is active in the toolbox.

▪ If it is hidden, show the **Formatting** toolbar by activating the **Formatting (Form/Report)** option under the **View - Toolbars** command.

▪ Select the control(s) concerned.

The control can be a text box.

▪ On the **Formatting** toolbar, click the appropriate alignment tool button:

to left-align the text.

to centre the text within the control.

to right-align the text.

Modifying the font and text style

* Show the form or report concerned in Design view (⬚) and make sure the ⬚ tool button is active in the toolbox.

* Select the control(s) concerned.

* To change the font, open the drop-down list on the [Arial ▼] tool then click the name of the font you wish to apply to the text in the selected control(s).

* To change the font size, open the list on the [10 ▼] tool then click the value that corresponds to the character size you want to apply to the text in the selected control(s).

* To change the style, or text attributes, click the appropriate tool buttons on the **Formatting** toolbar:

  B   to apply/cancel **bold** type.

  I   to apply/cancel *italics*.

  U   to apply/cancel <u>underlining</u>.

* To change the colour of the text, open the list on the [**A** ▼] tool button and click the colour you wish to apply to the text in the selected control(s).

* Save the changes made to the form or report then close it.

All of these features can also be found in the property sheet of the selected control:

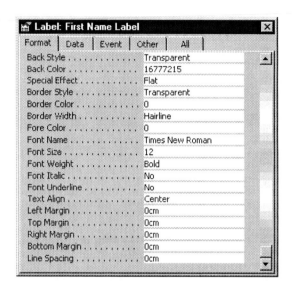

Certain properties offer more options than can be found on the ***Formatting*** *toolbar:*

- the ***Distribute*** option in the ***Text Align*** property justifies the text.

- the ***Font Weight*** property contains several options for changing the boldness of text characters.

⑥ ▪ Changing the presentation of controls/sections

▪ Show the form or report concerned in Design view and make sure the ⌨ tool button is active in the toolbox.

▪ If it is hidden, show the **Formatting** toolbar by activating the **Formatting (Form/Report)** option under the **View - Toolbars** command.

▪ Select the control(s) concerned or click the section title to select it.

The section title bar changes colour.

▪ To change the background colour, open the list on the 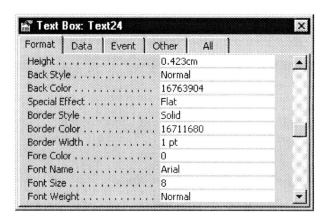 tool then click the background colour that you want to apply to the selected control(s) or section.

▪ To change the colour of a control's outline, open the list on the tool then click the colour you wish to apply to the outline of the selected control(s).

*If the **Transparent** option is active, the selected colour will not be visible.*

▪ To change the thickness of a control's outline, open the list on the tool then click the button that corresponds to how wide you want the selected control's outline to be.

▪ To alter the appearance of a control, open the list on the tool then click the type of look (shadowed, raised etc) you want the selected control(s) to have.

▪ Save the changes made to the form or report and close it.

All of these features can also be found in the property sheet of the selected control(s):

Text Box: Text24	
Format	Data	Event	Other	All
Height	0.423cm
Back Style	Normal
Back Color	16763904
Special Effect	Flat
Border Style	Solid
Border Color	16711680
Border Width	1 pt
Fore Color	0
Font Name	Arial
Font Size	8
Font Weight	Normal

*In the property sheet you can also use the **Border Style** property to choose a different style for the control's outline.*

*You may notice that the tool buttons on the **Formatting** toolbar represent the last option chosen. To apply this option to another control, you can simply click the tool button without having to open the list of options.*

7 ▪ Changing the format of the values in a control

▪ Show the form or report concerned in Design view (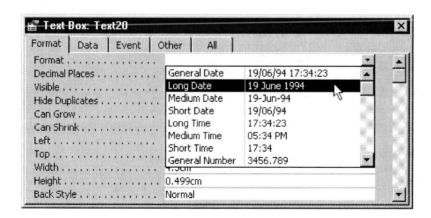) and make sure the tool button is active in the toolbox.

▪ Select the control concerned then click the tool button to display its property sheet.

▪ Click the **Format** tab then in the **Format** property, select the required format from the drop-down list.

Text Box: Text20		
Format	Data	Event	Other	All
Format		
Decimal Places	General Date	19/06/94 17:34:23
Visible	Long Date	19 June 1994
Hide Duplicates	Medium Date	19-Jun-94
Can Grow	Short Date	19/06/94
Can Shrink	Long Time	17:34:23
Left	Medium Time	05:34 PM
Top	Short Time	17:34
Width	General Number	3456.789
Height	0.499cm	
Back Style	Normal	

The list of formats available depends on the authorised data type used in the field.

▪ If required, give the number of decimal places to use, in the **Decimal Places** property.

※ Save the changes made to the form or report and close it.

8 ▪ Showing/hiding sections

※ Show the form or report concerned in Design view (⊡▾) and make sure the ⬚ tool button is active in the toolbox.

※ Open the **View** menu to activate or deactivate the **Page Header/Footer** and/or **Form** (or **Report**) **Header/Footer** options.

※ If you try to hide sections that contain controls, Access displays a message to inform you that all the controls will be deleted. Click **Yes** to hide the sections and delete the controls or **No** to cancel hiding the sections.

※ Save the changes made to the form or report and close it.

9 ▪ Changing the height of a section

※ Show the form or report concerned in Design view (⊡▾) and make sure the ⬚ tool button is active in the toolbox.

※ Point to the top of the next section's title bar.

The mouse pointer adopts the same form as it does when you modify the height of a row or width of a column.

※ Drag upwards or downwards, depending on whether you want to decrease or increase the height of the section.

※ Save the changes made to the form or report and close it.

📄 *Data in the Page Header and Page Footer sections appear at the top and bottom of each page in the form or report.*
Data in the Form (or Report) Header and Form (or Report) Footer sections appear on the first page of the form (or report) or on the last page.

Below you can see **Practice Exercise** 5.2. This exercise is made up of 9 steps. If you do not know how to complete one of the steps, go back to the lesson to refer to the corresponding title. When you have finished, check your work by reading the **Solution** on the next page.

Steps that are likely to be tested in the exam are marked with a 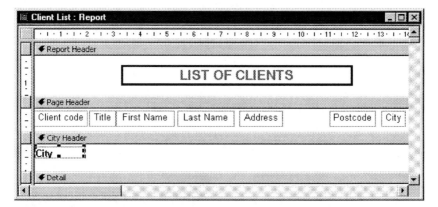 symbol. It is however recommended that you follow the whole exercise in order to gain a complete understanding of the lesson.

☞ Practice Exercise 5.2

*To work through exercise 5.2, open the **5-2 BookBase.mdb** database located in the **MOUS Access 2000** folder.*

1. Select all the controls in the **Detail** section of the **Client List** report.

⊞ 2. Move the **City** text box and its label from the **City Footer** section into the **City Header** section then save the changes made to the report.

3. Delete the **City** label from the **City Header** section then move the **City** text box as shown below:

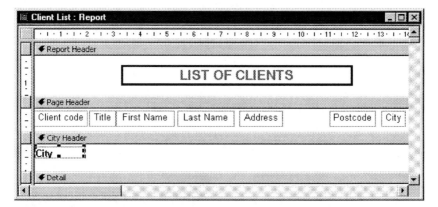

Save the changes made to the report.

4. Widen the **City** text box by **4 cm** (1.5 in) and increase its height by **0.5 cm** (0.2 in) in the **City Header** section then save the changes made to the report.

5. Change the presentation of the text in all the controls in the **Page Header** section, following the instructions below then save the changes made to the report:

   - apply a centred alignment.

   - apply the **Times New Roman** font in size **12**.

   - apply **bold** type and a **dark blue** colour.

6. In the **Page Footer** section, change the presentation of the control that displays the page numbers, following the instructions below then save the report:

   - apply a light blue colour to the control's background.

   - apply a **1** point weight to the control's outline.

   - apply a dark blue colour to the control's outline.

7. Apply a **Long Date** format to the control that contains the current day's date in the **Page Footer** section (=now()). Save the changes made to the report then display it in **Print Preview** view. If necessary, zoom in on the current date to see it clearly then return to the report's design.

8. Hide the **Report Header/Footer** sections then save the report.

9. Reduce the height of the **Detail** section by about **1 cm** (or ½ in). Save the changes made to the report then close it.

If you want to put what you have learned into practice in a real document you can work on summary exercise 5 for the DESIGN VIEW section that can be found at the end of this book.

It is often possible to perform a task in several different ways, but here only the most efficient solution is presented. You can go back to the lesson if you wish to see the other techniques that can be used.

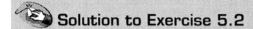

Solution to Exercise 5.2

1. To select all the controls in the Detail section of the Client List report, start by clicking **Reports** in the objects bar, select the **Client List** report then click the ⌨ Design button. In the vertical ruler, click at the same level as the top of the text boxes in the **Detail** section, then spread the selection by dragging down past the bottom edges of the controls in question.

2. To move the City text box and its accompanying label from the City Footer section into the City Header section, click the **City** text box in the **City Footer**. Click the ✂ tool button, click the title bar of the **City Header** section then click the 📋 tool button.

   To save the changes made to the report, click the 💾 tool button.

3. To delete the City label from the City Header section, click the **City** label in the **City Header** section then press the Del key.

   To move the **City** text box, point to one of its edges then drag it to the position shown in step 3.

   To save the changes made to the report, click the 💾 tool button.

4. To widen the City text box in the City Header section by 4 cm (1.5 in) and increase its height by 0.5 cm (0.2 in), click the **City** text box in the **City Header** section, if it is not already selected. Next, point to the sizing handle in the top right corner of the control and drag **4 cm** to the right and **0.5 cm** down.

To save the changes made to the report, click the 🖫 tool button.

5. To change the presentation of the text in all the controls in the Page Header section, click in the vertical ruler, at the same level as the top of the labels in the **Page Header** section. Drag downwards along the ruler, past the bottom edge of the labels to select them all.

To apply a centred alignment, click the ≡ tool button on the **Formatting** toolbar.

To apply Times New Roman font in size 12, open the drop-down list on the [Arial ▾] tool and click the **Times New Roman** option. Next, open the drop-down list on the [10 ▾] tool and click **12**.

To apply bold type and a dark blue text colour, click the [**B**] tool button then open the drop-down list on the [**A** ▾] tool and click the dark blue colour square.

6. To modify the control displaying page numbers in the Page Footer section, start by clicking that control to select it.

To apply a light blue background colour, open the drop-down list on the [🖉 ▾] tool and click the light blue colour square.

To apply a 1 point border to the control's outline, open the drop-down list on the [▾] tool then click the [□] tool button.

To colour the control's border blue, open the drop-down list on the [🖉 ▾] tool and click the dark blue colour square.

To save the changes made to the report, click the 🖫 tool button.

7. To apply a Long Date format to the control that contains the current day's date in the Page Footer section (=now()), click this control to select it. Click the 🖳 tool button to display its property sheet. Click the **Format** tab then select the **Long Date** option from the drop-down list on the **Format** property.

To save the changes made to the report, click the 🖫 tool button. To show the report in Print Preview view, click the 🔍 tool button.

If you need to zoom in on the date to see it clearly, position the pointer over that part of the page and click.

To return to the report's design, click the 📐 tool button.

8. To hide the Report Header/Footer sections, click the **View** menu, deactivate the **Report Header/Footer** option then click **Yes** to confirm deleting the sections with the controls they contain.

To save the changes made to the report, click the 🖫 tool button.

9. To increase the height of the Detail section by 1 cm (about ½ in), point to the top edge of the title bar of the **City Footer** section and drag **1 cm** upwards.

To save the changes made to the report, click the 🖫 tool button then activate the **File - Close** command.

QUERIES
Lesson 6.1: Queries

1 ▪ **Creating a single table query**

Queries are a way of selecting records according to one or more criteria. Queries can be saved and run at any time; when you run a query, Access selects the records in the query's source table that meet the set criteria.

*This type of query is called a **select query**.*

Without a wizard

※ There are three ways of creating a query without the help of a wizard:

- click **Queries** in the objects bar then click the [New] button on the database window,

- click **Queries** in the objects bar then click the **Create query in Design view** shortcut,

- open the drop-down list on the **New Object** ([icon]) tool button then click the **Query** option.

*The **New Query** dialog box does not appear when you use the **Create query in Design view** shortcut.*

※ Select the **Design View** option and click **OK**.

※ Click the tab in the dialog box that corresponds to the type of object you wish to use for the query.

※ Select the name of the object you wish to add to the query.

※ Click the **Add** button then click **Close**.

*The top part of the window shows the list of fields in the source table. The lower part, called the **design grid**, is where you define your criteria. You can change the height of either of these sections by dragging the horizontal line that separates them.*

※ Insert into the design grid the fields that you want to display in the datasheet (the query results). To do this, double-click each field name or drag each field towards the design grid. You can also open the drop-down list that appears on the **Field** row of the design grid and choose the field name from the list.

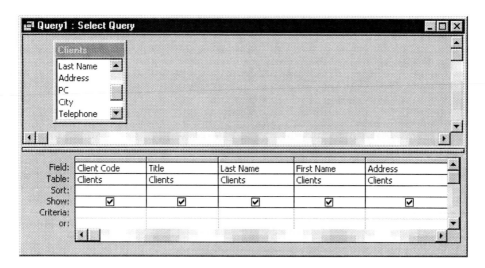

You can see the check boxes on the **Show** row are ticked automatically.
The name of the table used appears in the **Table** row of the design grid,
providing the **Table Names** option is active in the **View** menu.

» Give the selection criterion (or criteria) in the **Criteria** row, placing them in the
column of the field on which they are based (cf. Setting query criteria).

» You can set a criterion on a field but not show that field in the results; in this
case, deactivate the **Show** check box.

» For each field on which you wish to set a sort order, click the corresponding
column on the **Sort** row then select either an **Ascending** or **Descending** sort
order.

*If you want to use several sort keys, place the first field to be sorted furthest on
the left, then the second to be sorted and so on.*

» To see the query's result, go into Datasheet view by clicking the ▦▾ tool
button or run the query with the ! tool button.

Query1 : Select Query						
Client code	**Title**	**Last Name**	**First Name**	**Address**	**City**	
AND01	Ms	Anderley	Suzanne	67 Milton Road	Abbeyville	
STA01	Mr	Stanes	Bill	3/28 Bartlett Cres	Abbeyville	
DRE01	Ms	Drew	Joanne	78 Abbey Road	Abbeyville	
DOR01	Mrs	Dorcas	Michelle	10 Kings Ct	Beecham	
YOU01	Mr	Youmad	Malik	58 Eagle St	Beecham	
LIN03	Ms	Lindstrom	Julie	86 Clarence St	Cleveden	
UND01	Mrs	Underov	Natasha	7/19 Clarks Road	Cleveden	
SAL01	Ms	Salakis	Helen	85 Kessler Avenue	Cleveden	
TOW01	Mr	Townsend	Andrew	8 Waterford Dr	Eastport	
STO03	Mr	Stone	Stephen	56 Lawrence St	Eastport	
BUR01	Mr	Burton	James	37 Chambers St	Eastport	
JOH01	Mr	Johnson	Ian	19 Playton Place	Eastport	

Record: |◄ ◄ | 1 | ► ►| ►* | of 52

This datasheet can be used like any other datasheet based on a table. You can modify its presentation (column width, row height, etc) but you can also modify the data it contains and these changes will be carried over automatically into the source table.

The tool button can be used to return to the query's Design view.

⁎ You can save a query in Design or Datasheet view. To do this, activate the **File - Save** command or 🖫 or ⌷Ctrl⌷ **S**.

⁎ If necessary, close the query with the **File - Close** command.

📄 *You can interrupt a query that is running by pressing* ⌷Ctrl⌷⌷Break⌷.

To change the title of a column in the result datasheet, enter the name of the field on which it is based in the design grid with this syntax: ***column name:field name***.

With a wizard

▪ There are three ways of creating a query using a wizard:

- click **Queries** in the objects bar then click the ⊞ New button on the database window,

- click **Queries** in the objects bar then click the **Create query by using wizard** shortcut,

- open the drop-down list on the **New Object** tool button (⊞ ▾) and click the **Query** option.

The New Query dialog box does not appear if you use the Create query by using wizard shortcut.

▪ Select the **Simple Query Wizard** option and click **OK**.

▪ In the **Tables/Queries** list box, select the table or query on which your new query will be based.

Access displays a list of all the fields in the chosen table or query.

▪ Insert the fields you want to use in the query:

- to insert a field, click it in the **Available Fields** list and click the ＞ button.

- to insert all the fields, click ＞＞ .

- to remove one of the fields you just selected, click it in the **Selected Fields** list and click the ＜ button.

- to remove all the selected fields, click the ＜＜ button.

You can also insert a field into the query by double-clicking it.

▪ Click the **Next** button to go to the next step.

▪ If you want the query to group certain records to make statistical calculations, activate the **Summary** option. Otherwise, leave the **Detail** option active.

▪ Click **Next**.

- Enter the title that should appear on the query's title bar.

  This title is also the name under which the query will be saved.

- Choose one of the options depending on whether you wish to go straight to the result datasheet or to the query's structure in Design view.

- Click the **Finish** button.

- To show the query in Design view, to modify its structure, click the [⊻▾] tool button.

  *The **View** button ([▦▾]) can be used to return to Datasheet view.*

- Proceed as you would if you were creating the query without a wizard.

▣2 ▪ Managing the query design grid

- Click **Queries** in the objects bar, select the query concerned and click the [⊻ Design] button.

- To remove one or more fields from the query design grid, select it by clicking the field selector that appears over the field name and press [Del]. To remove all the fields from the grid, use the **Edit - Clear Grid** command.

- To add all the fields in a table into the design grid, double-click the table's title bar then drag the selection onto the **Field** row in the design grid.

  *You can also drag the * symbol from the first row of the field list onto the design grid. This instructs the query to select all the fields from the table. However, if you want to set criteria on any of these fields, you must insert them again individually then deactivate the **Show** option on the duplicate fields (otherwise they appear twice in the result sheet).*

- To move a field, point to the field selector then click to select it. Drag the field selector: a thick vertical line appears. Place this line in the position where you wish to put the field.

▪ To insert a field into the design grid, select it in the table then drag it towards the design grid. Choose in front of which field you wish to place it and drag it onto that field.

▪ Click the ⊞ tool button to save the changes made then close the query with the **File - Close** command.

> The **Insert - Rows** command inserts a new row of criteria above the active row. The **Insert - Columns** command inserts a new column to the left of the active column.

3 ▪ Running a query

▪ There are two ways of running a query:

- if you are in the database window, double-click the icon of the query you want to run.

- click **Queries** in the objects bar, select the name of the query you want to run, click the ⌨ Design button then the ❗ tool button.

The query extracts the records from the table that meet the set criteria.

▪ If necessary, close the query datasheet window by clicking the ✕ button.

⊞4 ▪ **Setting query criteria**

Setting a criterion according to field type

▪ Open in Design view (⬚ ▾) the query in which you wish to set a criterion.

▪ On the **Criteria** row, click the column that corresponds to the field where you want to set the criterion. Enter your criterion according to the following principles:

Field type	How to set criteria	Examples
Number, Currency or AutoNumber	enter just the value, without any formatting.	1500.45
Date/Time	enter the date or time in the format of your choice; the data may be typed between # signs.	01/01/00 >#01/01/00# 01 January 2000 01-Jan-2000
Yes/No	to select values corresponding to Yes,	enter: Yes, True, On or -1
	to select values corresponding to No,	enter: No, False, Off or 0

▪ Click the ⬚ tool button to view the result.

▪ Save the changes made to the query by clicking ⬚ then use the **File - Close** command to close it.

Using operators

* Show the query in Design view (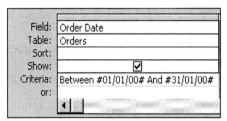) then click the **Criteria** row in the column of the field on which you want to set your criteria.

* Set the criterion using the comparison operators (there are six of them): < (Less than), <= (Less than or equals), > (Greater than), >= (Greater than or equals), = (Equals), <> (Different from).

* Other operators can also be used in Access:

Operator	Selects records	Examples
Between	with a field value that falls between two given values.	Between "A" and "C" Between 10 and 20 Between 01/01/00 and 02/02/00
In	with field values that are included in a given list.	In ("BERLIN"; "PARIS")
Is	with a blank or nonblank field.	Is Null Is Not Null
Like	with data corresponding to an approximate criterion.	Like "*ave*"
Not	with data that does not meet the criterion.	Is Not Null Not In ("BERLIN"; "PARIS")

Here are some examples:

Field:	Order Date
Table:	Orders
Sort:	
Show:	☑
Criteria:	Between #01/01/00# And #31/01/00#
or:	

selects the orders placed between the 1st and 31st of January 2000.

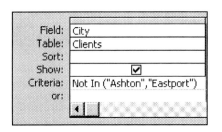

selects all the clients except those living in Ashton or Eastport.

※ Click the ! tool button to view the result.

※ Save the changes made to the query by clicking the 🖫 tool button then close it with the **File - Close** command.

> 📄 Criteria expressions can also contain functions (in this case, field names must be placed in square brackets). For example: Year([Date of birth])=1966 selects all the recorded people born in 1966.

> 🔍 If you are entering a very long criterion, you can press Shift F2 to display the **Zoom** window. You can also increase the width of the column where you are entering the criterion by dragging the line that separates the two field selectors.

Setting criteria concerning different fields

There are two possible situations:

- you want to extract the records that meet all the criteria at once: you should link the criteria with the AND operator,

- you want to extract the records that meet just one or another of the criteria: you should link the criteria with the OR operator.

※ Show in Design view (🖉 ▾) the query in which you wish to set several criteria referring to different fields.

* If the criteria should all be checked simultaneously, insert them all <u>in the same row</u>, in the columns representing the corresponding fields.

This query selects all the male clients ("Mr") living in Eastport.

* If one or other of the criteria has to be met, insert them in different rows.

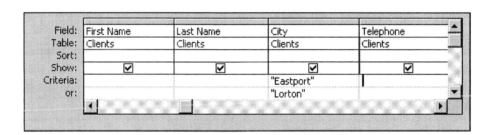

This query selects the clients living in either Eastport or Lorton.

* Click the ▣ tool button to view the results.

* Save the changes made to the query by clicking the ▣ tool button then close it with the **File - Close** command.

5 ▪ Inserting a calculated field in a query

* Show in Design view (▣) the query in which you wish to insert a calculated field.

* Click an empty space on the **Field** row.

※ Give the name of the calculated field followed by the corresponding expression. Use the form **Name:expression**.

Field:	Book Number	Retail Price	Quantity	Total Price: [Retail Price]*[Quantity]	
Table:	Order Lines	Order Lines	Order Lines		
Sort:					
Show:	☑	☑	☑	☑	
Criteria:					
or:					

The Total Price field calculates the price for each quantity of books ordered.

※ Click the [!] tool button to view the results.

※ Save the changes made to the query by clicking the [💾] tool button then close it with the **File - Close** command.

> 📄 *It is not strictly necessary to give the name of a calculated field. If none is given, Access gives the field a name such as Expr1.*

6 ▪ Calculating statistics without grouping

You can perform a statistical calculation on all the records in a table or on a group of records, selected with a set of criteria. For example: the number of clients in a table, or the number of clients living in a certain town.

※ Show in Design view ([📝▾]) the query in which you wish to make a statistical calculation without grouping (or if the query does not exist, create it).

※ In the query design grid, insert the field on which you wish to make your calculation.

※ Click the [Σ] tool button to display the **Total** row or use the **View - Totals** command.

*A second click on that tool hides the **Total** row.*

※ Click the **Total** row in the column concerned and in the list choose the type of statistical calculation you wish to use: **Sum**, **Avg**, **Min**, **Max**, **Count**, **StDev**, **Var**, **First** (which displays the first value in the table corresponding to a selected record) and **Last** (which displays the field's last value).

※ If they are not all inserted, insert the fields on which the selection criteria are based.

*Automatically, Access assigns the **Group By** operation to these fields.*

※ Choose the **Where** operation for these fields.

*The **Show** option is deactivated automatically.*

※ For each criterion you wish to set, click the **Criteria** row in the appropriate column and enter your criterion.

For example, how many male clients ("Mr") live in Rafter?

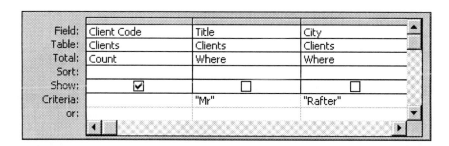

Field:	Client Code	Title	City
Table:	Clients	Clients	Clients
Total:	Count	Where	Where
Sort:			
Show:	☑	☐	☐
Criteria:		"Mr"	"Rafter"
or:			

※ Click the ![!] tool button to view the results.

※ Save the changes made to the query by clicking the ![save] tool button then close it with the **File - Close** command.

7 ▪ Calculating statistics on groups

There are three ways in which you might want to calculate statistics on a group of records:

- *you might perform one statistical calculation per group, without applying selection criteria (for example, how many clients live in each town?).*

- *you might perform a statistical calculation on all the records in the table, then select groups of records meeting certain criteria (for example, you count the number of clients per town then select the towns with more than 5 clients).*

- *you might select certain records then make the statistical calculation on those records only (for example, you select the clients who have placed an order since a certain date and count how many there are in each district).*

Calculating on all the records

- ※ Show in Design view the query on which you wish to make a statistical calculation on all the records.

- ※ In the query design grid, insert the field used to group the records.

- ※ Click the $\boxed{\Sigma}$ tool button to display the **Total** row and check that the operation proposed is **Group By**.

- ※ Insert the field concerned by the calculation into the query grid then open the **Total** drop-down list and choose the type of calculation you want to perform.

- ※ Click the $\boxed{!}$ tool button to view the results.

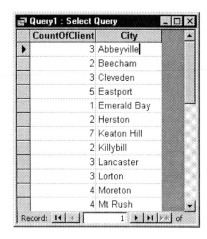

This datasheet shows the number of clients living in each town.

※ Save the changes made to the query by clicking the 🖫 tool button then close it with the **File - Close** command.

🔍 To select records according to the result of the statistical calculation, simply set the criteria in the column containing the said calculation.

Calculating on certain records

※ Show in Design view the query on which you wish to make a grouped statistical calculation on some of the records.

※ Insert into the query grid the field used to group the records.

※ Click the Σ tool button to display the **Total** row and check that the proposed operation is **Group By**.

※ Insert into the query design grid the field on which the statistical calculation is based then in the **Total** drop-down list, choose the calculation operation you wish to perform.

» Insert into the grid the field(s) on which the selection criteria are based and then select the **Where** operation for these fields.

» Give the selection criteria.

For example, this query counts the number of clients, per city, whose first contact with the company was before 31 May 2000.

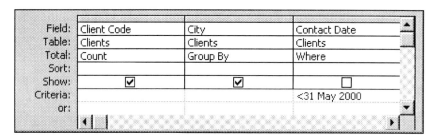

Field:	Client Code	City	Contact Date	
Table:	Clients	Clients	Clients	
Total:	Count	Group By	Where	
Sort:				
Show:	☑	☑	☐	
Criteria:			<31 May 2000	
or:				

» Click the ! tool button to view the results.

» Save the changes made to the query by clicking the 🖫 tool button then close it with the **File - Close** command.

🕮8 ▪ Creating a multiple table query

With a wizard

» If you have not already done it, establish the relationships between the tables you want to use in your multiple table query.

» There are three ways you can create a multiple table query with a wizard:

- click **Queries** in the objects bar then click the ⟦🗗 New⟧ button on the database window,

- click **Queries** in the objects bar then click the **Create query by using wizard** shortcut,

- open the drop-down list on the **New Object** tool button (⟦🗗 ▾⟧) and click the **Query** option.

*The **New Query** dialog box does not appear when you use the **Create query by using wizard** option.*

※ Select the **Simple Query Wizard** option then click **OK**.

※ In the **Tables/Queries** list, select the table or query from which you want to create the new query.

Access displays a list of all the fields in the chosen table or query.

※ Insert the fields you want to use in the query:

- to insert a field, click it in the **Available Fields** list and click the [>] button.

- to insert all the fields, click [>>].

- to remove one of the fields you just selected, click it in the **Selected Fields** list and click the [<] button.

- to remove all the selected fields, click the [<<] button.

You can also insert a field into the query by double-clicking it.

※ In the **Tables/Queries** list, select the second table or query you want to insert into the query.

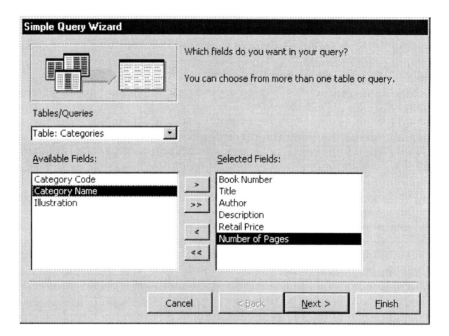

- In the same way, insert the fields from this second table or query into the **Selected Fields** list, making sure the same fields do not appear twice.

- Proceed in the same way to insert any fields from other tables or queries.

- Click the **Next** button to go to the next step.

- If you want the query to group certain records to make statistical calculations, activate the **Summary** option. Otherwise, leave the **Detail** option active.

- Click **Next**.

- Enter the title that should appear on the query's title bar.

  This title is also the name under which the query will be saved.

- Choose one of the options depending on whether you wish to go straight to the result datasheet or to the query's structure in Design view.

- Click the **Finish** button.

※ If you want to subsequently see the query in Design view, to work with the query design grid, click the 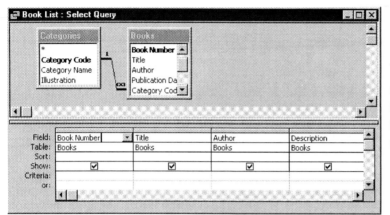 tool button.

*The **join line** that links the two tables represents the relationship that exists between them.*

※ Work with the query design grid as you would for a single table query.

※ Click the ! tool button to view the results.

*By default, Access creates an **inner-join** relationship between the tables in the query. Only records with counterparts in the other table appear in the datasheet.*

※ Save the changes made to the query by clicking the 🖫 tool button then close it with the **File - Close** command.

Without a wizard

※ There are three ways you can create a multiple table query without using a wizard:

- click **Queries** in the objects bar then click the New button on the database window.

- click **Queries** in the objects bar then click the **Create query in Design view** shortcut.

- open the drop-down list on the **New Object** tool ( ) and click the **Query** option.

The New Query dialog box does not appear when you use the Create query in Design view shortcut.

※ Choose the **Design View** option and click **OK**.

※ Click the tab that corresponds to the type of object you want to use in the query.

※ Select the names of the objects you wish to add to the query. To select several adjacent objects, click the first name then drag over the others. To select several nonadjacent objects, click the first object name then hold down the Ctrl key while you click the others.

※ Click the **Add** button then click the **Close** button.

You can also double-click an object's name to add it to the query.

If the two tables have already been linked in the Relationships window, a join line will now appear between them. If not, Access will create a join line automatically if it can find a common field within the two tables.

※ Work with the query design grid as you would for a single table query.

※ Click the tool button to view the results.

※ Save the changes made to the query by clicking the tool button then enter the **Query Name** in the appropriate text box then click **OK**.

※ Close the query with the **File - Close** command.

The Query - Show Table command or can be used to insert a new table into the query.

9 ▪ Using a query to delete records

Creating a delete query

▪ Start by creating a select query that will extract the records you require.

▪ Click the ▣ tool button to check the list of extracted records.

▪ Click the ▣ tool button to return to the query in Design view.

▪ To transform a select query into a delete query, use the **Query - Delete Query** command or open the drop-down list on the ▣ tool to select the **Delete Query** option.

A ***Delete*** row appears in the query design grid and the ***Show*** row disappears.

▪ If you wish, save the query by clicking the ▣ tool.

Running a delete query

▪ If you are in the database window, double-click the name of the query: the icon of this type of query contains an exclamation mark.

If you are in Design view, click the ▣ tool button.

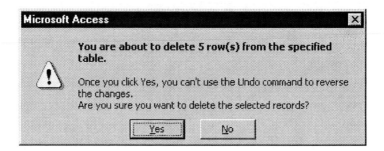

▪ Click the **Yes** button to confirm deleting the records.

 You can interrupt a query while it is running by pressing Ctrl Break.

10 ▪ Using a query to update records

▫ Start by creating a select query that will extract the records you require.

▫ Click the 🔲 tool button to check the list of extracted records.

▫ Click the 🔲 tool button to return to the query in Design view.

▫ To transform a select query into an update query, use the **Query - Update Query** command or open the drop-down list on the 🔲 tool to select the **Update Query** option.

*An **Update To** row appears in the grid while the **Show** row disappears (this type of query does not display the records).*

▫ On the **Update To** row, go to the column of the field whose values you wish to update and enter the expression that will modify those values:

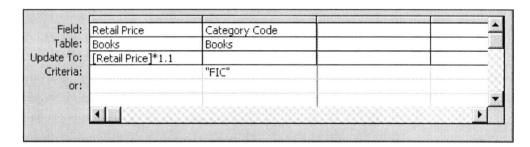

This query will increase by 10% the price of the products in the FIC category.

▫ Click the 🔲 tool button to update the records.

▫ Click **OK** to confirm the update.

▫ Save the changes made to the query by clicking the 🔲 tool button then close it with the **File - Close** command.

Below you can see **Practice Exercise** 6.1. This exercise is made up of 10 steps. If you do not know how to complete one of the steps, go back to the lesson to refer to the corresponding title. When you have finished, check your work by reading the **Solution** on the next page.

Steps that are likely to be tested in the exam are marked with a ▦ symbol. It is however recommended that you follow the whole exercise in order to gain a complete understanding of the lesson.

☞ Practice Exercise 6.1

To work through exercise 6.1, open the **6-1 BookBase.mdb** database located in the **MOUS Access 2000** folder.

1. Without using a wizard, create a query in which you insert, in this order, the fields **Client Code**, **Title**, **Last Name**, **First Name**, **Address**, **City** and **Telephone** from the **Clients** table. Sort this query by the **City** field in ascending order then display it in Datasheet view to see the results. Go back into the query's design then save it under the name of **Client List**.

▦ 2. Make the following changes to the **Client List** query then save the changes made:

- remove the **Address** and **Telephone** fields from the query design grid,

- insert the **Has Account** field before the **City** field,

- move the **First Name** field before the **Last Name** field.

3. Run the **Client List** query then close it.

4. In the **Most Recent Clients** query, set a criterion that will extract the list of all the clients whose first contact date comes after June 30, 2000. Run the query, save it then close it.

In the **Books Without Description** query, set a criterion that will extract the list of books that do not have a description: ensure that the **Description** field is not visible in the datasheet of the query results. Run the query, save it then close it.

In the **Southern Clients** query, set criteria that will extract the list of clients living in **Stoughton** and **Tewesbury**. Run the query, save it then close it.

5. In the **Order Lines by Book** query, insert a calculated field that you can call **Total Price** and which will show the total for each book ordered. Run the query, save it then close it.

6. Create a query that will add up the number of female clients (by the title Mrs or Ms). Save the query as **Female Clients** then run it and close it.

7. Create a query that will add up the number of clients, per city who were clients before 31 May 2000 (by their contact date). Save this query as **Pre-May 2000 Clients by City**, run it then close it.

8. Using a wizard, create a query that you will call **Book List** and in which you should insert (in this order) the fields **Book Number**, **Title**, **Author**, **Description**, **Retail Price** and **Number of Pages** fields from the **Books** table and the **Category Name** field from the **Categories** table. Next, go into the query's design to sort the list in ascending order by the **Book Number** field then place the **Category Name** field after the **Description** field. Save the changes made to the query, run it then close it.

9. Create a query that will delete the records from the **Eastern District Clients** table whose **City** field value is **Hollywell**. Run the query then close it without saving it.

10. Create a query that will increase the value of the **Retail Price** field by **10%** for all the books in the **FIC** category in the **Books** table. Save this query as **Increase FIC Books Price by 10%** then run and close the query.

If you want to put what you have learned into practice in a real document you can work on summary exercise 6 for the QUERIES section that can be found at the end of this book.

It is often possible to perform a task in several different ways, but here only the most efficient solution is presented. You can go back to the lesson if you wish to see the other techniques that can be used.

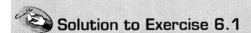

Solution to Exercise 6.1

1. To create (without a wizard) a query containing, in this order, the Clients table fields Client Code, Title, Last Name, First Name, Address, City and Telephone, start by clicking **Queries** in the objects bar then double-click the **Create query in Design view** shortcut. If necessary, click the **Tables** tab, select the **Clients** table, click the **Add** button then the **Close** button. Double-click, in this order, the fields **Client Code**, **Title**, **Last Name**, **First Name**, **Address**, **City** and **Telephone**.

   To sort this query in ascending order by City, click the **Sort** row, in the **City** column then open the drop-down list and choose the **Ascending** option.

   To show the query in Datasheet view to see the results, click the ⊞▾ tool button.

   To return to the query's design and save it under the name of Client List, click the ✎▾ tool button then click 💾. Enter **Client List** in the text box then click **OK**.

2. To remove the Address and Telephone fields from the design grid of the Client List query, select the **Address** field with its field selector (click just above the field name) then press the ⎄Del key. Next, select the **Telephone** field by clicking its field selector and press ⎄Del again.

   To insert the Has Account field before the City field in the design grid of the Client List query, drag the **Has Account** field from the table into the query design grid, onto the **City** field.

To move the First Name field before the Last Name field, select the **First Name** field by clicking its field selector then drag the field until the vertical line that appears is positioned between the **Last Name** and **Title** fields.

To save the changes made to the query, click the ⊞ tool button.

3. To run the Client List query, click the 🔲 tool button.

   To close the query, activate the **File - Close** command.

4. To set a criterion in the Most Recent Clients query that will extract the list of all the clients whose first contact date comes after June 30, 2000, start by clicking **Queries** on the objects bar. Select the **Most Recent Clients** query, click the 🖉 Design button then set the criterion as shown below:

Field:	First Name	Last Name	City	Contact Date
Table:	Clients	Clients	Clients	Clients
Sort:				
Show:	☑	☑	☑	☑
Criteria:				>30 June 2000
or:				

Click the 🔲 tool button to run the query. Click the ⊞ tool button to save the query then close it with **File - Close**.

To set in the Books Without Description query a criterion that will extract the list of books that do not have a description, start by clicking **Queries** in the objects bar and select the **Books Without Description** query. Click the ![Design] button then set the criterion as shown below:

Field:	Title	Author	Description	Re
Table:	Books	Books	Books	Bo
Sort:				
Show:	☑	☑	☑	
Criteria:			Is Null	
or:				

Deactivate the **Show** check box in the **Description** column, to ensure that the **Description** field is not visible in the datasheet of the query results. Click the ! tool button to run the query. Next, click the 💾 tool button to save it and close the query with **File - Close**.

To set criteria in the Southern Clients query that will extract the list of clients living in Stoughton and Tewesbury, click **Queries** in the objects bar and select the **Southern Clients** query. Click the ![Design] button and set the criteria as shown below:

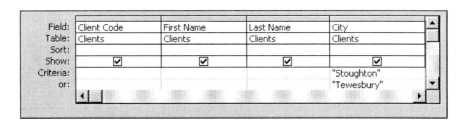

Field:	Client Code	First Name	Last Name	City
Table:	Clients	Clients	Clients	Clients
Sort:				
Show:	☑	☑	☑	☑
Criteria:				"Stoughton"
or:				"Tewesbury"

Click the ! tool button to run the query. Next, click the 💾 tool button to save it then close the query with **File - Close**.

▦ 5. To insert into the Order Lines by Book query a calculated field called Total Price and which will show the total for each book ordered, click **Queries** in the objects bar then select the **Order Lines by Book** query. Click the [▨ Design] button then insert the calculated field as shown below:

Field:	Retail Price	Quantity	Total Price: [Retail Price]*[Quantity]
Table:	Order Lines	Order Lines	
Sort:			
Show:	☑	☑	☑
Criteria:			
or:			

Click the [!] tool button to run the query. Next, click the [🖫] tool button to save it then close the query with **File - Close**.

6. To create a query that will add up the number of female clients (Mrs or Ms), click **Queries** in the objects bar then double-click the **Create query in Design view** shortcut. Select the **Clients** table, click the **Add** button then click **Close**.

Double-click the **Client Code** and **Title** fields to insert them into the design grid then click the [Σ] tool button to display the **Total** row. In the **Client Code** column, click the **Total** row then open the drop-down list and select the **Count** function. Next, in the **Title** column, click the **Total** row, open the list and select the **Where** option. Click the **Criteria** row in the **Title** column and enter **Mrs**. Press [↓] to go to the second criteria row (the **or** row) in the same column and enter **Ms**.

To run the query, click the [!] tool button.

To save this query as Female Clients, click the [🖫] tool button, enter the name **Female Clients** and click **OK**.

To close the query, activate the **File - Close** command.

7. To create a query that will add up the number of clients per city who were clients before 31 May 2000, start by clicking **Queries** in the objects bar then double-click the **Create query in Design view** shortcut. Select the **Clients** table, click first the **Add** button then **Close**.

Double-click the **Client Code**, **City** and **Contact Date** fields to insert them into the design grid. Click the Σ tool button to display the **Total** row. Click the **Total** row at the **Client Code** column then open the drop-down list and choose the **Count** function. Click the **Total** row at the **Contact Date** column open the drop-down list and choose the **Where** operation. Leave the **Group By** option selected in the **Total** row on the **City** column. Click the **Criteria** row in the **Contact Date** column and enter **<31 May 2000**.

To save the query, click the tool button, enter **Pre-May 2000 Clients by City** as the query name then click **OK**.

To run and close the query, click the tool button then use the **File - Close** command.

8. To create, using a wizard, a query called Book List and insert the fields as described in step 8 of the exercise, click **Queries** in the objects bar then double-click the **Create query by using wizard** option. Open the **Tables/Queries** list and select the **Books** table. Double-click the **Book Number**, **Title**, **Author**, **Description**, **Retail Price** and **Number of Pages** fields (in that order) in the **Available Fields** list. Open the **Tables/Queries** list again and select the **Categories** table. Double-click the **Category Name** field in the **Available Fields** list. Click the **Next** button twice, enter the text **Book List** in the text box then click the **Finish** button.

To sort by the Book Number field in ascending order, click the tool button to see the query's design. Click the **Sort** row in the **Book Number** column, open the drop-down list and select the **Ascending** option.

To move the Category Name field after the Description field, select the **Category Name** field by clicking its field selector (above the field name) then drag the field until the vertical line that appears is placed between the **Description** and **Retail Price** fields.

To save the changes made to the query, click the ⊞ tool button then click the ⓘ tool button to run the query.

To close the query, use the **File - Close** command.

9. To create a query that will delete the records for Hollywell from the Eastern District Clients table, start by clicking **Queries** in the objects bar. then double-click the **Create query in Design view** shortcut. Select the **Eastern District Clients** table, click the **Add** button then click **Close**. Double-click the **City** field to insert it into the design grid then click the **Criteria** row in the **City** column and enter **Hollywell**. Click the ⓘ tool button to check that the list of records you want to delete only contains records with **Hollywell** in the **City** field. Click ⊠ ▾ to return to the query design.

Activate the **Query - Delete Query** option then click the ⓘ tool button to run the query. Click the **Yes** button to confirm deleting the 5 records from the **Eastern District Clients** table.

To close the query without saving it, activate the **File - Close** command then click the **No** button on the message asking you whether or not to save the changes made to the query's design.

10. To create a query that will increase the value of the Retail Price field by 10% for all the books in the FIC category in the Books table, click **Queries** on the objects bar then double-click the **Create query in Design view** shortcut. Select the **Books** table, click the **Add** button then the **Close** button. Double-click the **Retail Price** field then the **Category Code** field to insert them in the query design grid. Next, click the **Criteria** row on the Category Code column and enter **FIC**. Click the [!] tool button to check that the list of records to be updated only contains books with **FIC** as the Category Code then click the tool button to go back to the query design.

Activate the **Query - Update Query** command, click the **Update To** row in the **Retail Price** column then enter the expression **[Retail Price]*1.1**.

To save the query, click the tool button, enter the query name as **Increase FIC Books Price by 10%** and click **OK**.

To run the update, click the [!] tool button then click **OK** to confirm updating the 29 records in the **Books** table.

To close the query, use **File - Close**.

SUMMARY EXERCISES

Summary Exercise 1   MANAGING DATABASES

Open the **Summary1.mdb** database, which is in the **Summary** folder in the **MOUS Access 2000** folder.

Display the database objects in the form of a simple list.

Delete the **Addresses** table and rename the **Sales Registered per Vendor** query as **Vendor Sales**.

Save the **Products** table as a Web page. You should save this page under the name of **Product List** in the **Summary** folder that is in the **MOUS Access 2000** folder.

The corrected database is saved as **Solution1.mdb**.

Open the **Summary2.mdb** database, which is in the **Summary** folder in the **MOUS Access 2000** folder.

Create an **Orders** table, without using a wizard, using the table below to guide you:

Field Name	Data Type	Description
Order Number	Number	Individual order number
Date	Date/Time	Date order placed
Paid	Yes/No	Has the order been paid?
Vendor Number	AutoNumber	Vendor number as seen in the Vendors table

The **Order Number** field should be used as the primary key.

Change the design of the **Orders** table in the following ways:

- insert a **Client Code** field, with a **Text** data type, beneath the **Date** field,

- move the **Paid** field after the **Vendor Number** field,

- choose a **Number** data type for the **Vendor Number** field.

Modify the properties of some of the fields in the **Orders** table as shown below then save the changes made and close the table:

- make it compulsory to enter data in the **Date** and **Client Code** fields,

- the **Client Code** field should be **5** characters long,

- The **No** value should appear in the **Paid** field each time a new record is created.

Create a lookup column containing the values **Mr**, **Mrs** and **Ms** for the **Title** field in the **Clients** table. The label for this lookup column should be **Title**.

Create, using a wizard, an input mask for the **Contact Date** field in the **Clients** table. Choose a **Medium Date** type of mask and make the # sign the placeholder character in the text box. Save the changes made to the **Clients** table and close it.

In the **Products** table, set a primary key made up of the **Category Code** and **Product Code** fields then save the changes made to the table and close it.

Establish a relationship between the **Products** and **Categories** tables, enforcing referential integrity.

Insert the **Clients** and **Orders** tables into the relationships window then relate these two tables, enforcing referential integrity and allowing field updates.

Modify the relationship that exists between the **Products** and **Categories** tables so as to allow field updates then save and close the relationships window.

Print the database relationships then close the window without saving it. Finish by closing the relationships window.

The corrected database is saved as **Solution2.mdb**.

MANAGING DATA

Open the **Summary3.mdb** database, which is in the **Summary** folder in the **MOUS Access 2000** folder.

Enter the following records into the **Clients** table then close the table:

Client code	Title	Surname	Address	City	Postcode	Contact Date	District
PRE02	Mr	PRENTICE	4, Ladybird Lane	CLAYFIELD	6700	03/07/00	Three Rivers
YOU01	Ms	YOUNG	18, Norton Terrace	RAYBURN	6200	04/07/00	Mapleton

Go to the **Clients** table's datasheet and make the following changes:

- widen the **Address** and **District** columns,

- move the **District** column in front of the **Contact Date** column,

- freeze the **Client Code** column,

- save this layout then close the **Clients** table.

Enter these two records using the **Enter Products** form then close the form:

Category Code	Product Code	Group	Product Details	Export	Unit Price	Tax Rate
VID	301	Video Recorder	VHS Pal/Secam, long play	No	299	10.50
VID	302	Video Recorder	VHS 4 head Pal/Secam/Nicam Stereo	No	399	10.50

Go to record **38** in the **Clients** table then delete it.

Sort the records in the **Clients** table in ascending order by **City** then filter the records to extract all the clients living in **Mapleton** or **Redfern** districts. Show all the records in the table again.

In all the addresses in the **Clients** table, replace the text **Ave** by the word **Avenue** (respect the same combination of upper and lower case letters).

Modify the page setup of the **Clients** table following these indications:

- apply a **10** mm (about ½ in) margin on the left and right of each page.

- print the column headings.

- give the pages a **Landscape** orientation.

Print two copies of the table (complete copies, not printed in groups of single pages) then close it.

In a new table that you can call **Vendor Info**, import the data from the **Info** worksheet in the **Vendors.xls** workbook, which is located in the **Summary** folder within the **MOUS Access 2000** folder. While importing the data, you should:

- use the column headings as field names,

- change the **Surname** field to **Vendor Name**,

- set the **Vendor Number** field as the primary key.

The corrected database is saved as **Solution3.mdb**.

Summary Exercise 4   CREATING FORMS AND REPORTS

Open the **Summary4.mdb** database, which is in the **Summary** folder in the **MOUS Access 2000** folder.

Using a wizard, create a form based on the **Addresses** table, following the guidelines below, then close the form:

- all the fields in the **Addresses** table should be added to the form,

- the form should have a columnar layout,

- the form should adopt a **SandStone** style,

- the text **Client Addresses** should appear in the form's title bar.

Associate the **Clients** table with the **Client Addresses** form then save and close the form.

Insert the **Products Subform** into the **Categories** main form. Position it **3** cm (1 ¼ in) into the **Detail** section, as shown below:

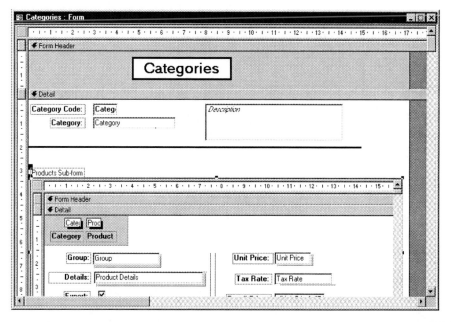

The default display view for the subform should be **Datasheet** and you should ensure that its data cannot be modified or deleted. Save the changes made to the main form (**Categories**), display it in **Form** view (show the form window full screen if necessary). Scroll through the first three records then close the form.

Using the wizard, create a report based on the **Clients** table, using the following guidelines:

- all the fields from the **Clients** table should be added except the **Observations** field,

- records should be sorted in **ascending** order by **District**,

- the fields in the report should be laid out one under the other, in **Landscape** orientation and each record should fit within the width of one page,

- the **Corporate** style should be used in this report,

- the text **Client Addresses** should appear in the report's title bar.

Define a sort order for the records in the **Client Addresses** report, sorting by **District** then by **City** then by **Surname**, each in ascending order. Next, group the records on the **District** field, with an interval value of 1. Save the changes made to the **Client Addresses** report then display it in **Print Preview** view to see the results.

In the **Client Addresses** report, use the **Northern District** query to print just the list of clients from the northern Redfern district. Save the changes made to the **Client Addresses** report then display it in **Print Preview** view to see the results. Print two complete collated copies of the report then close it.

The corrected database is saved as **Solution4.mdb**.

Open the **Summary5.mdb** database, which is in the **Summary** folder in the **MOUS Access 2000** folder.

Go into the design of the **Enter Orders (Main Form)** form and insert a **Date** text box under the **Order Number** text box.

Insert the **Paid** field as an option button as shown below:

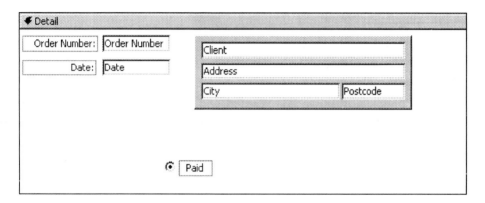

Create a combo box with a wizard. Take into account the following instructions:

- the combo box should be inserted beneath the **Date** text box,

- the **Client Code** and **Surname** fields from the **Clients** table contain the values you need to include in the box,

- the column containing the key values should be visible,

- the **Client Code** column contains the value that should be stored in the database,

- the **Client Code** field is the field in the form source in which you should store the value,

- the text in the list box label is **Client Code**.

Save the changes made to the form then display it in **Form** view. Open the **Client Code** list box to see its contents then return to the form's design.

Using a wizard, insert an option group along these guidelines:

- the option group should be inserted below the **Client Code** label as shown here:

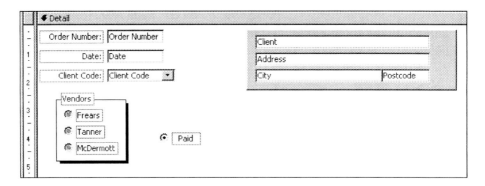

- the labels for the option group are **Frears**, **Tanner** and **McDermott** in that order,

- the active option by default is **Tanner**,

- the value **1** is assigned to the **Frears** option, the value **2** to the **Tanner** option and the value **3** to the **McDermott** option,

- the **Vendor Number** field is the field in which the value selected in the option group should be stored,

- use an **Option Button** type of button with a **Shadowed** style,

- the label for the option group is **Vendors**.

Save the changes made to the form then display it in **Form** view. Scroll through the first three records, to see the option group then display the form's design again.

Create a label with the text **ORDER FORM** in the page header, as shown below:

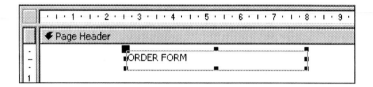

Draw a line above the text box that contains the total amount as on the illustration below:

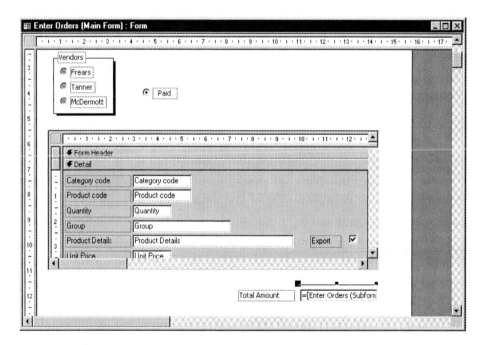

Save the changes made to the form then close it.

Go to the design of the **Enter Orders (Subform)** form.

Below the **Unit Price** text box, create a calculated control called **Pre-Tax Total** which will calculate the total price before tax of each product ordered. Apply a **Currency** format to this calculated control then choose an automatic tab order for the fields in the **Detail** section. Save the changes made to the form and display it in **Form** view. Go to record **3** to see if the control expression is correct then close the form.

Display the **Illustrated Category** form in **Form** view then activate the **Illustration** tab.

Insert two bound objects, **cassette.bmp** and **photo.bmp** that are in the **Summary** folder within the **MOUS Access 2000** folder, following these instructions:

- the **cassette.bmp** object should be inserted in the first record and the **photo.bmp** object should be inserted in the second record,

- for each object, establish a link between the Access document and the object.

Save the changes made to the form then close it.

Go to the **Client Addresses** report in **Design** view.

Move the **District** text box and its associated label from the **District Footer** into the **District Header** section.

Delete the **District** label from the **District Header** section then move the **District** text box as seen here:

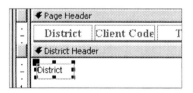

Increase the size of the **District** text box in the **District Header** section by **3 cm** (1.2 in) in width and **0.5 cm** (0.2 in) in height.

Change the presentation of the text in all the controls in the **Page Header** section, following these instructions:

- apply a centred alignment,

- apply the **Times New Roman** font in size **11**,

- apply a **dark green** colour.

Apply a light green background colour to the **Detail** section.

Reduce the height of the **District Header** by about **1 cm** (1/2 in).

Insert a page break so each new group starts on a new page. Show the report in **Print Preview** view, adjust the zoom then scroll through the first three pages. Save the changes made to the report then close it.

The corrected database is saved as **Solution5.mdb**.

Summary Exercise 6   QUERIES

Open the **Summary6.mdb** database, which is in the **Summary** folder in the **MOUS Access 2000** folder.

Without using a wizard, create a query in which you will insert, in this order the **Category Code**, **Product Code**, **Group**, **Product Details** and **Tax Rate** fields from the **Products** table. Sort this query in ascending order on the **Product Details** field then display it in **Datasheet** view to see the result. Return to the query design and save it as **Product List**.

Make the following changes in the **Product List** query then save the changes:

- insert the **Unit Price** field before the **Tax Rate** field in the design grid,

- remove the **Group** and **Tax Rate** fields from the design grid,

- move the **Product Code** field in front of the **Category Code** field,

Run the **Product List** query then close it.

In the **Clients Contacted Before May** query, set a criterion that will extract the list of clients contacted before 1 May 2000. Run this query, save it then close it.

In the **Client List Except Beeston and West Illing** query, set a criterion that will extract the list of all the clients except those living in Beeston or West Illing. Run this query then save and close it.

In the **Male Clients from Clayfield or Rayburn** query, set criteria that will extract the list of "misters" (male clients) living in Clayfield or Rayburn. Run this query then save and close it.

Create a query that will count the number of clients living in the Three Rivers district. Save the query as **Three Rivers Clients** then run it and close it.

Create a query that will count the number of clients by district whose contact date is >31 May 2000. Save this query as **Clients Contacted Since May 2000** then run it and close it.

Using a wizard, create a query called **Categories and Products**. Insert in this query (in this order) the **Category** and **Description** fields from the **Categories** table and the **Category Code, Product Code, Group** and **Product Details** fields from the **Products** table. Move the **Category Code** field in front of the **Category** field. Save the changes made to the query, run it then close it.

Create a query that will delete from the **Clients** table all the records with a **Contact Date** value before May 1, 2000. Save the query as **Delete Clients Contacted <May**, run the query then close it.

Create a query that will increase the value of the **Unit Price** field by **5%** for products in the **ACC** category in the **Products** table. Save the query as **Update 5% on ACC Products**. Run it then close it.

The corrected database is saved as **Solution6.mdb**.

MOUS Access 2000 Exam Objectives				
Tasks	**Lessons**	**Pages**	**Exercises**	**Pages**
Planning and designing databases				
Determining appropriate data input for your database	Lesson 1.2 Title 1	18	Exercise 1.2 Point 1	27
Determining appropriate data output for your database	Lesson 1.2 Title 1	18	Exercise 1.2 Point 1	27
Creating table structure	Lesson 2.1 Title 1	40	Exercise 2.1 Point 1	57
Establishing table relationships	Lesson 2.2 Title 1	64	Exercise 2.2 Point 1	72
Working with Access				
Using the Office Assistant	Lesson 1.1 Title 2	14	Exercise 1.1 Point 2	15
Selecting an object with the objects bar	Lesson 1.3 Title 2	32	Exercise 1.3 Point 2	36
Printing database objects (tables, forms, reports, queries)	Lesson 3.3 Title 2	119	Exercise 3.3 Point 2	121
Moving within records in a table, query or form	Lesson 3.1 Title 6	82	Exercise 3.1 Point 6	92
Creating a database (with a Wizard or in Design view)	Lesson 1.2 Title 1	18	Exercise 1.2 Point 1	27
Creating and modifying tables				
Creating tables with the Table Wizard	Lesson 2.1 Title 1	40	Exercise 2.1 Point 1	57
Setting primary keys	Lesson 2.1 Title 6	55	Exercise 2.1 Point 6	58
Modifying field properties	Lesson 2.1 Title 3	46	Exercise 2.1 Point 3	58
Using multiple data types	Lesson 3.1 Title 4	81	Exercise 3.1 Point 4	92

Tasks	Lessons	Pages	Exercises	Pages
Modifying tables in Design view	Lesson 2.1 Title 2	45	Exercise 2.1 Point 2	57
Using the Lookup Wizard	Lesson 2.1 Title 4	50	Exercise 2.1 Point 4	58
Using the Input Mask Wizard	Lesson 2.1 Title 5	53	Exercise 2.1 Point 5	58
Creating and modifying forms				
Creating a form with the Form Wizard	Lesson 4.1 Title 2	125	Exercise 4.1 Point 2	135
Using the control toolbox to add controls	Lesson 5.1 Titles 1 to 12	160 to 182	Exercise 5.1 Points 1 to 12	183 to 189
Modifying format properties (font, font size, colour, caption etc) of controls	Lesson 5.2 Titles 5 to 7	203 to 207	Exercise 5.2 Points 5 to 7	210
Using form sections (headers, footers, detail)	Lesson 5.2 Titles 8 and 9	208	Exercise 5.2 Points 8 and 9	210
Using a calculated control in a form	Lesson 5.1 Title 5	167	Exercise 5.1 Point 5	186
Viewing and organizing information				
Using the Office Clipboard	Lesson 3.2 Title 1	98	Exercise 3.2 Point 1	110
Switching between object views	Lesson 1.3 Title 4	34	Exercise 1.3 Point 4	36
Entering records with a datasheet	Lesson 3.1 Titles 1 and 5	76 and 82	Exercise 3.1 Points 1 and 5	91 and 92
Entering records with a form	Lesson 3.1 Titles 3 and 5	80 and 82	Exercise 3.1 Points 3 and 5	91 and 92

EXAM OBJECTIVES

Tasks	Lessons	Pages	Exercises	Pages
Deleting records from a table	Lesson 3.1 Title 7	85	Exercise 3.1 Point 7	92
Finding a record	Lesson 3.2 Title 4	107	Exercise 3.2 Point 4	114
Sorting records	Lesson 3.1 Title 8	86	Exercise 3.1 Point 8	92
Applying and removing filters (filter by form and filter by selection)	Lesson 3.1 Title 9	87	Exercise 3.1 Point 9	93
Specifying criteria in a query	Lesson 6.1 Titles 2 and 4	220 and 222	Exercise 6.1 Points 2 and 4	237 and 238
Displaying related records in a subdatasheet	Lesson 2.2 Title 3	70	Exercise 2.2 Point 3	72
Creating a calculated field	Lesson 6.1 Title 5	225	Exercise 6.1 Point 5	238
Creating and modifying a multi-table select query	Lesson 6.1 Title 8	230	Exercise 6.1 Point 8	238
Defining relationships				
Establishing relationships	Lesson 2.2 Title 1	64	Exercise 2.2 Point 1	72
Enforcing referential integrity	Lesson 2.2 Title 1	67	Exercise 2.2 Point 1	72
Producing reports				
Creating a report with the Report Wizard	Lesson 4.2 Title 1	142	Exercise 4.2 Point 1	154
Previewing and printing a report	Lesson 4.2 Title 3	150	Exercise 4.2 Point 3	155
Moving and resizing a control	Lesson 5.2 Titles 2 and 4	200 and 202	Exercise 5.2 Points 2 and 4	209 and 210

Tasks	Lessons	Pages	Exercises	Pages
Modifying format properties (font, font size, colour, caption etc)	Lesson 5.2 Titles 5 to 7	203 to 207	Exercise 5.2 Points 5 to 7	210
Using the control toolbox to add controls	Lesson 5.1 Titles 1, 5, 7, 8, 10, 11, 12	160 and 167 172 to 173 176 to 182	Exercise 5.1 Points 1, 5, 7, 8, 10, 11, 12	183 and 186 to 189
Using report sections (headers, footers, detail)	Lesson 5.2 Titles 8 and 9	208	Exercise 5.2 Points 8 and 9	210
Using a calculated control in a report	Lesson 5.1 Title 5	167	Exercise 5.1 Point 5	186
Integrating with other applications				
Importing data to a new table	Lesson 3.2 Title 3	105	Exercise 3.2 Point 3	110
Saving a table, query or form as a Web page	Lesson 1.3 Title 3	34	Exercise 1.3 Point 3	36
Adding hyperlinks	Lesson 3.2 Title 2	100	Exercise 3.2 Point 2	110
Using Access tools				
Printing database relationships	Lesson 2.2 Title 4	71	Exercise 2.2 Point 4	72
Backing up and restoring a database	Lesson 1.2 Title 3	25	Exercise 1.2 Point 3	27
Compacting and repairing a database	Lesson 1.2 Title 4	25	Exercise 1.2 Point 4	28

A

B

C

H

I

R

S

T

INDEX

U

UNBOUND CONTROL

UPDATE

V

VALUE

VIEW

W

WEB PAGE

▲ **Quick Reference Guide** ▲ **Practical Guide** ▲ **Microsoft® Approved**
▲ **User Manual** ▲ **Training CD-ROM** **Publication**

VISIT OUR WEB SITE http://www.eni-publishing.com

Please
affix
stamp
here

Ask for
our free brochure

**For more information
on our new titles
please complete
this card and return**

Name: ....

....

Company: ....

Address: ....

....

Postcode: ....

Town: ....

Phone: ....

E-mail: ....

ENI Publishing LTD

500 Chiswick High Road

London W4 5RG